From Millions to Millions and Millions More!

The 9 Rules
to Succeed in Network Marketing

KEITH HALLS

From Millions to Millions…and Millions More: The 9 Rules to Succeed in Network Marketing

Table of Contents

Acknowledgements

In all of my endeavors, I have surrounded myself with the best of the best to lead and inspire me.

I want to give a special thanks to Cherie Constance, my editor. She is a true wordsmith, and has been instrumental in the writing of this book.

I also must give a special thanks to Bill Halls, Cori Dyer and Krista Anderson. We are excellent business partners and the best of friends.

A very special thanks to Mr. Kaneko and Mrs. Ichigawa from Japan.

All in all, this book was only possible because of a lovely mother, Jane Halls, who supported me and always told me I could accomplish anything I set my mind to.

Last, but never least, to my beautiful and supportive wife, Heather, and our children Christina, Rebecca, Mark, Michael, Erica, Matthew and my grandson Logan. Thank you for a life worth living and a love worth having!

FROM THE DESK OF
KEITH HALLS

Dear Reader,

Margaret Thatcher once said, "Look at a day when you are supremely satisfied at the end. It's not a day when you lounge around doing nothing, it's when you've had everything to do and you've done it!"

If you want to get the most out of this book, you must:

1. Have the desire to change your current life trajectory
2. Have the objective to put each of the Rules in this book into planned action.

Many of us are the victims of "Self Help." We buy book after book, course after course, with the good intentions of altering our present to improve our future. Unfortunately, the books go untapped and the good intentions become past memories.

This cannot be one of those books.

Multi-level marketing (MLM), otherwise known as Network Marketing, is an active sport. You cannot passively join into this realm of business and hope for any measurable success.

Instead, you must actively and consistently pursue people to sponsor or clients to sell to. Although you must work hard to realize the kinds of success I talk about in this book, MLM allows you serious achievement that many 9-5 jobs lack. You set your hours, your schedule, and your level of accomplishment. In essence, you decide what success looks like to you!

This book gives you the step-by-step, rule-by-rule guide to getting the most out of MLM. Each chapter is a "Rule of the Game" designed to help you achieve long-term residual and leveraged income, the two benchmarks of true accomplishment in multi-level marketing.

I encourage you to read this book and then implement each "Rule" into your current MLM game plan. Although each of the "Rules" are crucial to your success, when combined into an action plan, you'll become an incredible ally to both your downline and upline.

To Your Ongoing Success,

Keith R. Halls

A journey of a thousand miles must begin with a single step.

– Lao Tzu

INTRODUCTION:
MY HUMBLE MLM BEGINNINGS

"Life without a purpose is a languid, drifting thing; every day we ought to review our purpose, saying to ourselves, 'This day let me make a sound beginning, for what we have hitherto done is naught!"

- Thomas Kempis

Hi. My name is Keith and I am a network marketing distributor. Sounds like I'm at an AA meeting right?

Well, according to the prestigious Keith Ray Halls survey, most people would rather go to the dentist or get audited by an IRS agent than sit across their kitchen table from a network marketer. You can picture it right? You've allowed an animated man or woman (usually a friend or family member) into your house for the evening and they're pointing to a chart with the downline circles and asking you to try the latest and greatest product.

But here's the deal. If you only knew what I knew, and had experienced the kind of wealth generation that I've experienced, you would know that Network Marketing or

Multi-level marketing (MLM) actually works. In fact, with the right know-how, it can work quite well! Yet, just like any other industry, in order to succeed, you need a "Rules of the Game" handbook. Luckily for you, you're one step ahead of the rest, because you're reading it right now!

The great thing about MLM is that you don't have to be a brain surgeon or a super athlete to succeed in life. In fact, with the power of MLM, you can make more money than many of them do, and have what they don't – time, financial freedom, and ongoing residual income. You can be an ordinary person, but make extraordinary wealth! By understanding the rules of MLM, you will have the power to succeed!

You don't have to reinvent the wheel; you just need to know where the tire store is. I honestly believe MLM is the greatest way to both share a great product and build wealth. I understand that this is a rather bold statement, but after you read my story, you'll see how a bit of boldness, mixed with a little bit of risk, and a whole lot of vision can culminate into a huge, ongoing reward.

Why I'm The Guy to Teach it to You

I am one of the only people in the entire world who has earned tens of millions of dollars on the corporate side of a successful MLM, only to leave it all and start over again as a distributor in yet another MLM. Starting all over again, from the ground up, I once again earned millions of dollars. I don't say this, or tell you how much I've earned, to brag. I tell you this to let you know that I have worked in the trenches on both sides and I know what it takes, from A to Z, to be successful. Because of this, I have the business chops to help you achieve your own financial goals in MLM. If your desire is to succeed and to make your own financial dreams come true in Network Marketing, then this book is exactly what you've been looking for. Just as importantly, every member of your downline needs to read this book to also benefit, which of course will help the greater good of the group as a whole.

Although, I have had to struggle and work hard, the end result has been financial freedom for me and my family, as well as sizeable commission checks that keep on coming and coming. I am extremely proud of my many successes, but they mean very little if they cannot benefit others. Network Marketing or multi-level marketing can have a very distinct and direct influence on your ability to make money. For those of you who are ready to achieve something great and are willing to put in the hard work to do so, then this is the one book that will give you the no-nonsense, candid steps to the process.

I have read too many books by people who have experienced limited success, yet promote themselves as "experts" on how to succeed in MLM. I am different; I've been there, done that and succeeded many times over! Bottom line: My formula works and my goal is to help you succeed too. So, let's begin.

My Humble MLM Beginnings

I grew up in a small town in East Texas named Nacogdoches. After high school, I got my first degree from a local university, called Stephen F. Austin University. Once I had completed my degree, I realized there were no (or very few) jobs available in my field (Political Science). So, I packed my bags, moved to Utah and attended Brigham Young University (BYU), which had one of the top five accounting programs in the United States. After graduating from BYU, I thought I was in the "sweet spot." I had a CPA degree from a prestigious university and a great job as an accountant. But there was this one, nagging problem—I was bored out of my mind! I hated crunching numbers in a cubicle for a company I had no stock or say in. My job neither drove me nor fulfilled me. By then, I had attended a university for over six years and I still didn't know what I wanted to be when I "grew up."

I began seriously thinking about my future and I decided I should become a lawyer. Not because I particularly loved the subject, but again, it had a nice ring to it. I was in the midst of preparing applications for various law programs and researching what law I would be interested in, when a late-night basketball game with a couple of friends changed my life and focus forever.

Being in the Right Place at the Right Time

It was one of those beautiful Utah Spring nights. After playing a few rounds of basketball, a good friend of mine asked if he could talk with me. We sat at one end of the court under the hoop and got into a deep conversation about what we were going to do with our lives. I thought my career opportunity (CPA and future Lawyer) sounded pretty impressive and I was kind of proud of it. I asked him what he was going to do. That one question, on that one night, changed all my "best laid" plans. He said that he and some others were starting a new Multilevel Marketing Company (MLM).

I had never heard of the term "Multilevel Marketing" or MLM before in my life. I think Nacogdoches, Texas may have been one of the few cities in the entire United States that even Amway hadn't invaded yet. I listened intently while he explained it all to me. I have to admit, it seemed a little whacky and unsustainable at first, but very soon, the excitement in his voice grew contagious. As I listened, I began to see the possibilities. One question he asked really stood out from all of the others. "Do you want to make something out of your life?" No one had ever asked me that before—certainly not my college career counselor. He asked it with such intensity and ferocity that I felt like it was up to me to finally answer it. If not now, then when?

He then asked me to be the accountant in the ground-floor operations of this start-up business and even though it seemed risky, it was the first thrilling offer I had ever had in my life. I believed in it so much that I gave up the chance to be a CPA/lawyer to join with them in the creation of a business wrapped in so much promise. In the beginning, I did their accounting on the side until it became a fulltime job. Although accounting and I had no love lost in the past, within this company, that dreaded field actually became fun because it finally had purpose behind it.

Of course, when I first joined, my excitement bubbled over into every conversation I had with family and friends. Many of them quickly tried to persuade me to quit. They thought I was venturing into very dangerous, uncharted territory and were worried I'd fail. However, if they had only been aware of what I knew back then, they would have known that I was on the precipice of something HUGE—the birth of a GIANT!

After a while, I became a stockholder in the company. Once again my parents and friends thought I had lost my mind because I had left my "secure future," borrowed money, and bought stock in some "no-name" company.

You're probably wondering who the company was. NuSkin (NUS on NYSE)! One of the largest Network Marketing Companies of all time. Of course, when I got involved back in 1984, no one could have guessed that this little start-up would grow to be such a mammoth in the industry.

I often think back to those early years, 1984-1990. What we did back then had never been done before and probably will never be done again in this industry. Can you imagine starting an MLM company with just $5,000? There were a lot of people who donated long hours and great amounts of mental and physical energy because, at our core, we all believed in it. Why? The only word I can use to describe it all was "excitement." We walked into the office KNOWING that each new day was full of personal growth, financial hope, and promise.

Of course, not everyone believed. People who didn't know us, or our story, doubted us. They thought we were all off our rockers. I can remember trying to open a bank account under the company's name. We would make appointments with bankers, who would either stand us up or laugh in our faces. Banks, potential suppliers, and other industry providers avoided us like the plague. Why? Because just as exciting as we were in our own eyes, bankers and suppliers saw us as simply another "flash in the pan" and told us to go get real jobs. Almost every step along the way, we were told, "You are too young and you will fail."

I can still remember a few years later, after we had become immensely successful and were the talk of the entire nation, those same bankers and suppliers, who had previously ignored us, were suddenly pleading to get appointments with us. We, however, stayed loyal to the people who helped us in those beginning days.

We had more than survived, we had thrived and won the game. With great products, an excellent compensation plan, and most importantly dynamic leadership, we broke the MLM mold!

On November 19, 1996, we took NuSkin public on the New York Stock Exchange and had one of the most successful IPO's of the year. The stock I had bought for $15,000, which was at the time a small fortune to me, sold in excess of $5,000,000! It's hard to explain how thrilling it was to watch some of the shares you bought in the beginning be sold for what seemed like the moon! To say the least, it was a very fruitful day for the original seven shareholders, who were once thought of as punk kids too big for their britches!

Back to the Drawing Board

Of course, that's not the end of the story. In fact, it was only the beginning. I worked at NuSkin for 17 years and when I left, I was one of the Senior Vice Presidents and a member of the Board of Directors. Those were 17 wonderful years, but I began to feel an itch and wanted to begin a new chapter in my life.

I decided to do the unthinkable. After leaving NuSkin, I opted to become the low-man on the totem pole. I chose to be a distributor in a different MLM Company. Which means I didn't start at the corporate level, with its perks, like corporate jets, insurance benefits, and big money. No, I entered in on the same playing field everyone else enters in at—as a plain 'ole distributor. You're probably asking yourself right now, "Why in the world would anyone in their right mind do something so crazy?"

It's a good and valid question. Even though I had made millions when we went public with NuSkin, I wasn't getting a residual paycheck coming to me for the rest of my life. That residual check, whether it's $500, $5,000 or $50,000 a month is something very few people ever achieve and I wanted it. So when I heard about a new and up-and-coming company with an offer to match bonuses on the people you sponsored, I was intrigued. I loved the compensation plan and the product. And by all intents and purposes, it looked like a homerun.

Great Success Often Comes From Failure

In the early days, I was beyond a shadow of a doubt, the worst distributor of all time. I could actually write an encyclopedia on how not to succeed in an MLM. If you were to take all the checks from the first 9 months of my work as a distributor, they would have been less than $3,000 total.

I made a lot of rookie mistakes. In particular, I remember the "dinner that never was." To deliver my pitch, I decided to have a formal dinner and ask all my closest friends over. I spared no expense on it. I had it professionally catered, had the house "spit-shined," and made sure all my kids knew that they had to be on their best behavior. I fretted over the menu, the seating arrangement at the table, and what I was going to wear. I practiced my presentation, made changes to it, and practiced again. So what was my fatal error? I basically told every single person I called that they were coming over for dinner and a "hard sale." Although I received confirmation from every friend, not one single person showed up. Lots of preparation, lots of food, and a whole lot of crickets chirping.

I was mortified.

Needless to say, I had failed in the eyes of many. And as I was failing I had a choice: I could either quit (the easy way out) or I could learn and work by "The Rules of the Game." I chose to work by the "Rules" and what a difference that choice has made to my life and bottom line.

After those first 9 months of apparent failure, things changed. I began earning real money—over $100,000 a month. Big difference, right? And the checks kept going up! Why? What had I done that caused such a drastic difference? I discovered and employed "The Rules of the Game" and applied them in my business and personal life.

After 5 years of huge success, I again decided to part ways. I joined yet another company and it has been another homerun. Just so I am not making any current income claims, I will not tell you how much I'm earning, but let's just say that once again I am doing extremely well. Why? It's easy! I'm just following "The Rules of the Game."

Unfortunately, no one teaches you these Rules. They are not taught in high school or college. I've spoken at numerous universities and I've served on Boards of Business Departments, and I have yet to see a class entitled "How to Succeed in Life" or "The Rules of the Game." The problem is that no one, as far as I know, teaches you what you need to know in order to succeed in life or in business. That is where "The Rules of the Game" come in; they teach you how to succeed. It is now your turn and your time to learn them and apply them.

The information written in this book, if placed into action can help set you and your team on the right path. But, just as in anything, it must be accompanied with massive action.

Before you jump in and join an MLM company, take a day or two to read this book. If you are already in an MLM company, take a break, read this book, and then make the necessary changes needed for great success. This book will guide you through some of the basic principles, or as I like to call them, "The Rules of the Game." What you're about to learn are some of the most important and closely guarded secrets to success in our industry.

But before we start on the rules, I need to teach you something that is very important about earning money.

Linear Income Vs. Residual and Leveraged Income:

Even though this isn't one of the Rules, you need to know the difference between linear and residual income. In this industry, it is one of the most important things for you to understand and take advantage of.

I'm not sure if any exact survey has ever been done, but I do believe that over 95% of all the people in the world earn their living through linear income. How do the rest of the people earn a living? They earn it through residual and leveraged income. Linear income takes place every time you exchange a unit of your time for a unit of money. For example, maybe you agree to work for $15.00 an hour or maybe you agree to work for $75,000 a year. Either way, you are exchanging a unit of your time for a unit of money. At the same time, you are also imposing a limit on how much you can earn. Why? Because there are only 24 hours in a day and there is only so much your boss is willing to pay you for that unit of time. Realistically, linear income is limited income—it's fixed. Even if you make a decent hourly wage or you receive a nice salary, you are limited. With linear income, you're putting a cap on what your time and effort are worth.

Residual income is different. Residual income creates wealth because it is based on the ability to continue receiving money for a sale or job, even though the work you did took place a long time ago. Some examples would be the interest on savings, royalties from writing a book, or commissions as a life insurance salesman. The list can go on and on, but, the biggest key is that residual income is not dependant on the amount you earn an hour or how many hours you work in a day. It's an ongoing amount paid for previous work and it can last as long as the source you built it from continues.

Another valuable component is leveraged income. Leveraged income is a little different. It's the ability to earn money from the efforts of others. A really good example of "leveraged income" is a large law firm. The senior partners in a big firm can earn many hundreds of thousands of dollars. It's not just because they bill at really high rates and put in really long hours (although generally both of those are true). It's because they are making an "override" on the hourly rates charged by all the junior attorneys and paralegals within the firm. Another good example is a computer software company that sells to businesses. Often, a salesperson's compensation is governed by the sales that person makes. But there is also usually a sales manager that receives a bonus based on whether the manager's team has met or exceeded its sales goals. The manager makes a little slice of every additional sales dollar brought in by the manager's sales team.

Both by themselves are excellent sources of income, but the maximum earning power lies in the combination of both residual and leveraged income.

MLM capitalizes on these two concepts. By recruiting another person to sell for your Company, the Company will pay you a commission. This allows you to leverage the time, energy and work of others and earn commissions when others sell. Long term residual and leveraged income is the goal of every network marketer; it is also the desire of every person who earns linear income. That ability to earn both residual and leveraged income is exactly what I'll be teaching you in this book.

A Real World Example of Linear Vs. Residual and Leveraged Income

To give you a good idea of the power behind residual and leveraged income, I'll tell you a little more about me and my life. You see, even though I have made millions in the MLM world, I have also been very successful in the Computer, Real Estate, and Bridal Business. (I know, I know, where did that last one come from, right?!)

Close to where my family lives, there was a clothing store that had the prettiest sweaters. Every year I bought sweaters for my mother, my sister, and daughters. Every time I went into the store, I offered to buy it from the owner. I figured, after buying all those sweaters, it would be a lot cheaper if I just owned the store. Every time I asked, the owner would smile and politely say no. She loved owning the store and working there.

In 1998, I was shopping for sweaters at the store and once again, offered to buy it. I was shocked when she actually said, "Yes!" We had lawyers write up the sales document and a few weeks later, I was the proud owner of a quaint, little sweater store. After the whirlwind of becoming the owner was over, I now owned a store, but didn't have a manager or any employees. Minor details, right? Of course, this presented a bit of a challenge for me, since at the time I was the Senior Vice President of NuSkin and extremely busy in the community.

On the day we signed the agreement, the former owner asked if I had given any thought to who would manage the store. I told her that I had given it a lot of thought, but I was still at a loss as to who the manager would be. She told me that her daughter, who had just gotten married, was looking for a job. She further explained that the store had been named after her daughter and that she had worked there since she was 15. Naturally, I was interested! So, the mother called her daughter and she and her new husband quickly drove over. After a short conversation, I hired her on the spot as the new manager and also gave her some stock as an incentive to get more sales.

About this same time, my 16 year old daughter was invited to the school prom. As a single father, raising two teenage daughters, you can only imagine how relieved I was when she told me that she wanted a dress that was "modest" and didn't show off too much of her body.

As we shopped in town, we were very surprised and disappointed that we couldn't find one "modest" dress for the prom. It was depressing. So we went to Salt Lake City, where there would be a bigger and more promising selection. Once again, we were greeted by the same result—lots of beautiful dresses, but not a single one that fit the "modest" bill. I ended up buying a dress, and then paying almost as much for alterations as we did for the dress! I was stunned that no one sold a modest, fashionable dress for prom, which produced one of those business "aha" moments. I saw a market niche and believed I could capitalize on it. As the marketing great Dan Kennedy always says, "There are Riches in Niches!"

The next week, I called a meeting with the management of my little store. I had decided that we would become the first "modest-only" retailer in our community. It sounded like a poor and risky business decision to others. I mean in a sex-driven society, who would open a store built solely on the idea of "covering girls up"? That and we were doing quite well in the sweater business, so why change the equation? I knew it would be a hard sale, and I was worried that my managers and employees would think I had simply lost it. Instead, my awesome team came back with a rather aggressive sales and marketing plan.

First, in order to make space for our new modest line of dresses, we marked down all of the sweaters in our inventory to half off. Next, we talked to middlemen about finding and buying "modest" dresses for the store. We couldn't find much, if anything. So, we started yet another business! Suddenly I was in the "designing" business, with the idea of also selling our dresses to other stores and customers throughout the United States. It was a bold endeavor, but we believed it would be a success.

By that time, I had invested a lot of money in this idea. The expansion of the business into the designer and distributor side would cost a lot more, and I was financing everything. After hiring the right team for our expansion, we had a meeting to decide who would get paid what amount. At the meeting, I carefully listened to each person as they made their request. I granted each the amount that they felt they were worth. Before the meeting ended, someone thought to finally ask me what I would like to receive for my business guidance, the funds for the operations, as well as other assorted duties. Because of my experience with NuSkin, I knew the power of residual and leveraged income. I told the group that all I wanted was a 2% commission on all the sales from all five companies for as long as I owned them. They thought I had lost my mind. I had put up a lot of money and time, and all I wanted was a measly 2% of sales. At that point, we weren't even sure we would have one sale and yet all I wanted was 2%—just 2 cents for every dollar that was sold.

Needless to say, our idea blossomed and we became one of the largest privately owned bridal, prom, and specialty wear sellers and distributors in the nation. We were also the largest "modest-only" clothing store in the United States. Within a few years, we had five separate companies; each one involved with some part of the process, from designing to the final retailing of the dress. Before long, we were selling millions and millions of dollars in dresses. My "silly idea" worked! And I was receiving 2% of ALL the sales from ALL five companies! Now, that's the power of residual, leveraged income!

My friends were able to get the salary they wanted and I was able to earn more than all of them put together and then some... and then some more. They chose linear income; I chose residual income. I made money whether I worked or not. They had set an income that was linear and thus put a cap on how much they could earn. I set an income that was residual and leveraged and because of this I received many, many times more. Why? I didn't place a cap on my income potential or worth. That is the power of residual, leveraged income and the reason why I, and so many other people, am attracted to the MLM industry.

At this point, I want you to ask yourself this question, "Am I truly earning what I'm worth?" If you can honestly answer a resounding and unswerving "yes," then maybe you don't need this book. But if you're like me and most people, you know that you're worth a lot more than what some company has deemed your value to be. When I worked as a CPA, I made pretty good money, but it was never fulfilling and I never felt like I was being paid what I was truly worth.

It's time for you to stop crunching the numbers, balancing the checkbook and waiting for that next paycheck to make it all better (for a while anyway) and use the power of residual and leveraged income to earn what you're worth! Today's the day and the "Rules of the Game" will show you the way!

The Rules are not listed in any exact order. They are all equally vital to you and your long-term success. Each one can help you succeed, but together they will make a powerful difference in your life and business. Remember, there are no guarantees, but if you learn and follow these nine rules, your chances are infinitely better.

Read the rules. Apply the rules. And you will succeed! Let's begin.

"Never let the odds keep you from doing what you know in your heart you were meant to do."

– H. Jackson Brown, Jr.

Rule One:
DREAM THE DREAM

The Dream Maker

"You can do it Keith," my mother used to say. "You can achieve anything you want to and you can help others do the same."

When I was young, I had some pretty lofty goals. According to my mother, by now I would be the President of the United States, I would have already cured cancer, and I would have beaten the greatest of the greats in basketball. As only a mother can, she listened to and shared in my dreams. I always loved talking to her about them, because she would usually say, "You can do that Keith, you can" and I believed her.

She would also say, "To succeed you need to work hard to make your dreams come true. You need to mix hard work, dedication, and a firm conviction to never quit." She taught me that if I helped others make their dreams come true; I would have loyal and dedicated friends and followers for life. One of the biggest keys in network marketing is being able to teach people how to dream big and then following through to show and help them to realize their dreams. To prosper in network marketing, it is essential that you help others to succeed.

Like everyone else, I have had door-to-door salespeople come to my home, trying to get me to buy one of their products so that they could win a trip to some exotic place or buy a new car. How motivated was I to spend my money, getting something of minimal value, just so someone else could win a new car? It was next to zero. I wanted a new car too. Their approach was all wrong. For years I was taught, "help another person achieve their dreams and they will help you for life."

Write Down Your Dreams

My home office desk is scattered with what my kids call "junk," but there is one piece of paper that is so important that I keep it front and center. I also keep a copy of it in my wallet. It contains a list of my personal dreams and I carry it with me everywhere I go. Almost every day, as I work from my desk or reach into my wallet, I am reminded of my dreams. It has been shown time and time again that a goal written down is one step closer to a goal realized.

In the same respect, once a goal or dream is verbalized to others it becomes a real entity—something you have to be accountable for. Having those you wish to help understand and verbalize their dreams is a crucial step in aiding them to develop a plan to accomplish those dreams. In MLM, if their dreams come true, so do yours!

As I am enrolling a person, I ask them what their dreams and goals are and then I carefully write each one down. Next, I work with them to make a plan so we can achieve each of the objectives. I never tell them my dreams (unless they ask) and I never dwell on what it will do for me or how it will benefit me. I only talk about their aspirations. Any time they may feel a bit discouraged, I remind them of their dreams and try to motivate them to keep the dream alive.

About 7 or 8 years ago, I met, on several occasions, with a leader from another company. I really wanted her to join our Network Marketing company as a distributor. I thought she would be awesome at it. Each time I spoke with her about it, she would gently, but firmly, turn me down. You see, she was already doing well earnings-wise in her position, and she didn't want to risk her current paycheck by joining with our newer organization. Yet, I believed that if she joined our team, with her people-skills and her determination, she would earn much, much more.

So one day, I followed this very important Rule of the Game and asked her, "What do you really want out of life? Because, I believe deep-down you want to join with me, however; I feel like someone or something is holding you back."

The moment I said this, she began to cry. It was not the reaction I had expected from this high-powered executive and I was a little taken aback and worried that I had offended her. She then pulled out two well-worn items from her purse—a picture of her mother and a copy of her bank statement. She said, "Even though I am earning a lot of money, each month, after my expenses, I don't have enough left over." Tears were streaming down her face as she showed me the picture of her aged mother and then said, "Keith, my dream is to be able to buy a home for my mother and save for my family."

This was our defining "aha" moment! I looked into her eyes and told her that together we could make her dreams come true. As she listened, she began to believe in me. Her face turned from tear-stained and full of anguish to a face lit with joy and hope. We suddenly had a marriage of the minds and an important goal in common.

About a year later, I was with her when she stood in front of an audience of over 1,000 people. She proudly held up a picture of a new house she had purchased for her mother, and a copy of her savings account to show how much she had earned and saved.

A dream, combined with a powerful and compassionate upline (me) resulted in a brand new house for her mother. The best news: thousands of other people were also positively effected by this one woman's dream and accomplishment. Many joined our company because of her. Her dream came true and so did the dreams of many others—all because she decided her dreams were more important than her fears. As I helped make her dreams come true, some of my dreams also came true. In an MLM environment, there's a positive feedback loop. One dream realized can ultimately result in hundreds of dreams realized, all feeding back to the original dreamer. The good of the one is ultimately the good of all and vice-versa.

The Age of the Disappearing Dreamers

As mentioned before, I travel a lot in my job. I spend a lot of time in airplanes, hotels, and convention centers. I like to explore each new city I'm in. No matter where I am, whether it's at home in the United States or abroad, I'm always surprised by how many people I see who have given up on their hopes and dreams. You can see it in their eyes, the way they carry themselves, and the manner they approach others. Their childhood dreams have been beaten down and instead of working harder, they have simply given up. They have shut down their dream factory indefinitely.

I'm writing this book to show you that your dreams are valid and can come true. Whether you are 17, 27, 57, or even 97, you should continue dreaming and working toward your goals. If you combine your dreams with a plan, hard work, dedication, and a firm conviction to never quit, then many of your dreams can become a reality.

Remember your dreams, find out what you need to do to make them a reality, and then work with a determined attitude to eventually realize them. It is the first "Rule of the Game."

Worksheet # 1: Dreams

Dreams	*Goals*	*Date*
Save for retirement	1. Choose an investment counselor	June 1
	2. Determine How Much to Save	June 2
	3. Save $100 a Month	July 1
Build a big downline	1. Sponsor your first two members	June 1
	2. Teach your new members to sponsor two new people	June 1— Always!

Are You A Dream Chaser or A Dream Achiever?

As each of us start to realize the potential and the power of our dreams, we also need to remember that we can either be "dream chasers" or "dream achievers." As Antoine de Saint-Exupery once said, "A goal without a plan is just a wish."

If you want to be a dream achiever there are many steps you

must take. To begin, list each of your dreams. You can't achieve your dreams if you don't plan and track what it is you are working toward. You may want to create a separate piece of paper for each dream and keep it in a binder. Next to your dreams, make a list of the goals you need to accomplish to realize those dreams. For example, you may dream of saving enough money for retirement. To make that dream come true, you need to list your goals, which could be:

• Select a Financial Planner at a reputable firm

• Determine how much you will need to invest

• Start saving

The final preparatory step is to determine the date when you will accomplish each goal. Establish the date and work to meet it.

Learn to Dream the Right Dreams

Another vitally important part of dreams is simply asking yourself, "what am I dreaming about?" If you are dreaming of fame, fortune and honors, the pursuit of them may dominate your life, but they will only bring temporary happiness. If you are dreaming of personal happiness and a sense of purpose, of helping others, and/or providing for your family, then your motivation to achieve them will be much stronger.

Dream my friends. These dreams can be one of your most valuable assets. Work toward them and happiness and success will be your reward.

It's Your Turn!

The importance of goal setting cannot, for one minute, be underestimated. Unfortunately, many people do not put much stock in the action part of dreaming. This is obvious by how many people wander aimlessly from one job to another or one task to another.

Follow these steps to set your goals:

1. Make sure your goals are realistic but challenging.

2. Set goal time increments.

3. Use the following chart to write down your goals, and then figure out how you're going to achieve them.

Your 5 Year Plan

	I will have accomplished:	What habits or behaviors will I change to accomplish these goals:
By *Day 90*		
By *Day 180*		
By *Year 1*		
By *Year 3*		
By *Year 5*		

"I've come to believe that each of us has a personal calling that's as unique as a fingerprint—and that the best way to succeed is to discover what you love and then find a way to offer it to others in the form of service, working hard, and also allowing the energy of the universe to lead you."

– Oprah Winfrey, 2002

Rule Two:
BELIEVE

Everyone Is A Salesperson

We've all had the unfortunate experience of being the audience to a person who was selling us something that they could care less whether we bought it or not. You can see it by the bored look on their face and hear it in their ho-hum sales pitch. In return, you also could care less whether you buy the product or not. The result is that no sale takes place and no one's life is changed and better for it.

If you asked the person what went wrong with the presentation, he or she would most likely give this excuse, "I'm just not a salesperson." However, nothing could be further from the truth.

Whether we like to admit it or not, we're all salesmen and women. Think about how you had to "sell" yourself to get the first date with your spouse. You dressed up, put your best foot forward, and then you "sold" the dickens out of yourself! Or think about job interviews you've had. You did everything you could so that the person hiring would look at you and think you're the best person for the job. I could go on and on, but just believe me on this, we are all involved in the selling process each and every day of our lives.

If you want to succeed, make the sale, and/or sign up a new distributor, then you must believe. Believe in what? More than anything, you must believe in yourself. Everything else is a distant second. In order to succeed, it is vitally important in this "Rule of the Game" to have a strong belief system in yourself. If you don't believe in yourself, then chances are no one else will either and your odds of succeeding are very, very minimal. Why would I say that? Because true belief in yourself and a well-defined goal will spur you into action that very few people can or will want to reject.

Avoid the Dream Stealers

Unfortunately, just about all of us have "dream-stealers" in our life. A dream stealer is a person who will try to shake and destroy your belief system. Sadly, you don't have to look very far or very hard to find them. They are usually the people you know and trust the most and because of certain fears you may already have, these dream stealers can cause you to seriously doubt yourself, your product, and/or company.

Have you ever been excited about something and you couldn't wait to share it with your family, friends, or spouse? When they didn't understand, they immediately told you that your idea or dream was "silly" or "stupid," right? They questioned your intelligence and, in effect, destroyed your confidence.

After talking to one or two more dream stealers you probably decided to keep your mouth shut because you didn't want your friends or family to think that you were wrong. You became afraid of rejection, which ultimately forced you into inaction. Your confidence in yourself was crushed and you simply quit believing in your dream.

The fact is, we are in an industry which many people distrust. Therefore, you need to learn how to be proactive rather than reactive. Think of all the reasons that people may disagree with your choice in MLM. Next, write down some answers to each one of the objections. You will then have an arsenal of responses ready when the "dream stealers" come around. Here are a few examples I've heard once or twice:

1. MLMs are scams.

Multi-level marketing companies are not scams. True, their have been a few bad apples, but most MLMs are legitimate companies who operate in the light of day, and some are publically traded on the New York Stock Exchange. These companies allow ordinary people the rare chance to become their own boss, set their own hours, and do something they love and believe in.

2. No one really makes money.

Not true. People who strive to build their downline and encourage their team to do the same, experience success and ongoing commission checks. Of course there are always going to be people who join, collect product in their garage, and never work a day at it. You'll find that in any start-up type of business. But, for those people who consistently add to their downline, they find that their income builds as their team builds.

3. There is no science to support these products.

Most MLMs have researchers, chemists, and physicians on staff. Products are developed and tested with the utmost care for consumer safety and health. The product ingredients are rigorously tested and are shown to provide amazing health benefits.

Remember: People can argue with you about who has the best company, they can argue with you over who has the best products, however, the one thing they cannot argue with you about is who YOU are and whether or not YOU will succeed.

The second "Rule of the Game" is to believe. Let me share a story about a very close friend of mine that I have known most of my life.

When he was just a boy—he was kind, popular, and enjoyed sports. He was also the smartest boy in his class; maybe even in his whole school. His grades were always A's and he was consistently at the top of the class. Like other young men, he dreamed about what he was going to be when he grew up. One day he wanted to be a doctor and with his academic proficiency, he was well on his way to achieving this dream.

Unfortunately, he didn't have the necessary support system. At a young age, his life was filled with "dream stealers." Even though he had loving and caring parents, their dreams for him were quite different. They had other plans for him. Every time he succeeded and accomplished milestones toward his dream, his parents tried to point him in a different direction. Nobody was there along the way to encourage him toward his goals. I remember watching him and feeling so sorry for him and his lack of support.

Feeling pressured, he married at a very young age. This wasn't part of his dream, but at this point his whole belief system had been shattered. Unfortunately, the person he married was unsupportive. She often belittled him and told him that he would never succeed unless he followed the plan his parents had laid out. Before the age of 25, he was already broken.

After a while, the old spark of determination and passion reappeared. He began to work toward his dream again. As he gained back some of his belief system, he was able to prove to his family, friends, and wife what his future could and would be. He finally took his life back!

Within a few months, he was working in a major company's research and development department, helping to create new health products. He went back to school and got another degree and then another. It was inspiring and fascinating to watch him go from floundering to triumph in such a short time period, all because of one choice to stop believing the dream stealers and start believing in himself. He began to tape phrases up around his apartment reassuring him of his dream.

He put belief quotes up at work and he did the same at school. It wasn't easy, but nothing in this life, which is really worth anything ever is. He succeeded and is now helping others in the medical field. He is now a confident, happy, and compassionate person. Looking at him now, you would never believe he had once been "beaten down" by the "dream stealers." I could tell many stories of famous people who have overcome rejection and succeeded, solely because they believed in themselves. I use this "ordinary" story because sadly, it is a reflection of what many people are experiencing each and everyday.

So, #2 in the Rules of the Game is to not let the "dream stealers" steal your dreams and beliefs. Always remember that you are more than good, you are great and God's supreme creation. With that as a background, and the foundation found in this book, you can and will succeed. He believes in you, so shouldn't you?

I realize that in my life as a salesman, I will be rejected and rejected often—probably on a daily basis. However, I believe in myself and don't let rejection affect me. I am not sure of the exact number, but as a distributor in two different companies, I believe that well over 250,000 people have said yes to me or a member of my team. They believed in us and joined my downline. Knowing this is incredibly satisfying.

However, I also believe that well over 250,000 have said no to me or my team. That's okay too. It's all part of the game. I have been a distributor for about 3,000 days. That means that either I, or people in my downline, have experienced rejection over 85 times a day. WOW!!! With those figures, I would have good reason to believe I am a failure. Instead, I keep working, earn millions of dollars, accept the rejection, and learn to believe in myself more and more every day.

Of course, it is important to also build your belief system even further. You must also believe in your company, your product, and the compensation plan. To build and strengthen your belief system you must take time to study and learn about the products and the company each and every day. Listen to as many company-supported and upline calls as you can. I have been around the industry for a long time and it always amazes me how many people think (note I didn't say believe) that just by joining they will make more money than their doctor or lawyer. They "think" that all they have to do is sign up a few people and that it will duplicate without any further action. Nothing could be further from the truth. You have to build your belief system and the best way to do this is to study and work hard. Every day, I take time out of my busy schedule to study some aspect of the company or its products. I don't study all day; I usually just take 15-20 minutes. Maybe I learn more about the products or maybe about the company itself. I try to make sure that I learn enough, so that I can then make a persuasive presentation with confidence and a smile. Because of this effort, my audience, whether it's one person or 100 people, will know that I believe in what I do, which will make them infinitely more likely to join or buy from me.

I believe in me. I believe that I can and will help people. This belief system took a lot of determination and effort to build. But I paid the price and now I'm reaping the rewards! Just so you know, I believe in you! I believe that you can also succeed. Now, it's your turn to believe in yourself and follow this "Rule of the Game." Take action today by writing down your dreams and getting your belief system in yourself, the product, and the company set in stone.

Worksheet #2: Listen, Learn, And Live

To succeed, it is very important to write down your beliefs and why you believe in them. This list should be forever evolving. It will become your "Why" and "What."

• Why did I join?

• Why this company in particular?

• What am I expecting?

• What can I do to help others succeed?

The longer you are with a company, you'll find that you have more reasons to add to your belief list. Every time you learn something new, every time you go to a convention and discover new information, or every time you are speaking with another person and hear something that makes sense, write it down. You will never remember all you have learned or heard at last year's Convention, or from a Business Opportunity meeting you attended a month ago. By taking notes, you can look back over time and realize how much you have learned and why your belief system is so strong.

This is just a short, simple example, however it is important that you write down all of the things that help to enhance your belief system. The stronger your belief system, the greater your chances are of meeting with success.

What I Believe	Why I Believe
The Company	They have the vision to lead us into becoming a large, successful company
More money for retirement	I will save $250 a month from my MLM commission check
The Products	They have helped me lose 10 lbs. They are completely organic
The Compensation Plan	I earned $500 my first month.

It's Your Turn! Take a minute to fill out this chart with your "whats" and "whys." Make sure you're absolutely honest with yourself, otherwise it will be an exercise in futility.

What I Believe	Why I Believe

Understanding Yourself

These questions will help you discern your belief system:

The last time I felt...

The last time that I felt success was:_____

_____

The last time that I did something that I really, really didn't want to do, but did it anyway, was:_____

_____

The last time I felt truly happy was:_____

_____

_____

The last time I felt truly at peace was: _____

_____

_____

The last time I felt really proud of myself was:_____

_____

The last new skill that I developed was:_____

_____

The last time that I felt totally focused was:_____

_____

"I am financially free"

You have won the lottery and acquired millions and millions
of dollars. You don't have to worry about bills, loan repayments
or other payments. Picture this incredible wealth. Now, what
are you going to do? How are you going to fill each day?

_____

_____

_____

_____

_____

_____

_____

_____

_____

_____

"Real success is finding your lifework in the work that you love."

– David McCullough

THE KEITH HALLS STORY

Rule Three:
IT'S A BUSINESS...TREAT IT LIKE ONE!

Even though I was born in a small town in East Texas, I was the perfect fit for MLM and sales. Let me explain. While growing up, my mother and father taught me the importance of work and by the time I reached the age of 14, I was expected to find a job. Living in a small town made that difficult. The fact that it was also a college town, made it nearly impossible. But the rules had been set. So, I had to think of something to do.

Many of our neighbors (who were rich enough), would hire a company to come over once a week to mow and care for their lawns. The problem was that the people providing the service were not doing a very good job. I overheard our neighbors expressing their frustration about it to my Dad and I saw a window of opportunity open. I decided to start my own lawn care business and be the best lawn mower in the whole town. People would beg me to mow their yard! One Problem: no one was going to come to me. If I was going to make it, I would have to go door to door and ask them if I could be their yard guy. To do this, I wrote, practiced in front of the bathroom mirror, and memorized the best sales pitch in the whole world (at least it was in a fourteen year old mind).

I also had to decide how much to charge. With a minimal amount of research, I found out how much the other companies were charging: about $4.00 a yard. To determine my price, I did something a bit more scientific. I estimated how long it would take me to mow a lawn and then decided how many yards I could mow in a day. I did the mathematics and found that I needed to charge $5 per yard. Being a teenager, I had some serious financial needs!

My summer job started the same day school ended. In the zeal of advertizing my services and winning clients, I had overlooked some chief details. The morning of my first job, I had to actually ask my father to teach me how to do some of the important tasks, such as learning where to put the oil and gas and how to start the mower.

I had gathered enough clients to be busy from about 7AM to 7 PM, 6 days a week. The first day was brutal! It was hot and hard and even more importantly, I quickly found out that I HATED mowing lawns. The hot Texas sun, which shines intensely, beat down on me all day. After the second or third day, I was already dreaming about an exit strategy. But I knew it was all in vain because quitting was not an option in our house.

After about two weeks of lawn mowing-Hades, I got a phone call. One of my best friends was planning a swimming party at the local swimming pool the next day. He told me that over 10 people were coming, as well as the girl I had pined over in middle school. I had a real dilemma. I wanted to go SO BADLY; yet there was no way I could say yes to him. Most of my clients were allowing me to take care of their lawns only because they were friends with my parents. If I disappointed or neglected them, my parents would find out and probably ground me for life.

That's when I had my first business-related "aha" moment. I called another good friend, John, and subtlety sleuthed out whether or not he had been invited to the swimming party. He had not. I then casually asked if he wanted to earn some extra money mowing lawns. He not only accepted, he quickly thanked me. At the end of our conversation he asked me how much he would earn. I thought about it for 2 or 3 seconds and told him $4.00 (remember I was charging the clients $5.00). I let him know that I would check on the lawns, pick up the payment, and then drop his amount by his house later that day (he only lived about 500 yards away). Although he did the manual labor, I was the one that had set up the business and secured the clients. I was owed a certain amount for my effort and foresight.

In order to go swimming with my friends, I had him mow three lawns for me that day. At the end of the day, after swimming and playing with my friends, I made sure all the lawns were mowed and collected the money. I went to John's house and paid him the $4 per yard. As I walked home that night, I was so excited at this ingenious discovery. Not only had I made money that day without doing any work, I had also played and swam and basked in the presence of my "true love." This was so great I wondered if it was even legal.

However, all I was doing is what people all over this great country do every day; I had started my own business and hired an employee. Since that day worked out incredibly well, I asked John if he wanted a permanent job. I went out again and secured enough clients to keep both of us busy. By that time, I was really living the good life. I was making money from the lawns that I was mowing, and I was also making a little from the lawns John mowed. I continued to recruit new clients and soon had too many lawns for John and me to take care of. So I asked my 13 year old brother if he would like to earn some extra money. I told him the same thing I told John and he too was every bit as excited. When he asked me how much he was going to earn, I quickly replied, "$3.00." He was only 13 and thrilled about the prospects of working at all.

Even though I had never heard of MLM or the power of residual and leveraged income, that is exactly what I was doing. I learned at a very young age how to start my own business and how to earn money.

About 35 years later I was speaking to an audience in Houston. Who should be in the audience? John. While I told the lawn-mowing story, he quickly calculated how much money he thought I owed him, along with interest. He interrupted the presentation and presented me with the bill. The audience loved it and I tried to plead poverty!

Opportunity Costs

Consider this:

1. In 2006, MasterCard International reported that 40 percent of small business owners predicted their greatest expense would be payroll. The National Retail Federation expected that retail fraud would cost retailers $9.6 billion.

2. It was estimated that the average small business spends nearly $8,000 per employee to stay in compliance with government regulations.

3. It was also estimated that there were 23 million shoplifters in the United States, costing retailers more than $27 million dollars per day. And that was is 2006. Costs have most likely doubled since then.

Why all the harsh numbers? I referenced these stats to remind you that even though you are starting your own business when you first sign up to become a distributor, the signup fee and the costs to get started are usually quite minimal.

Most people would like to be their own boss and own their own business. In traditional business, if a person wanted to own their own business and be their own boss, he/she would possibly open a franchise, buy an existing business, or even put up a sign and start a business that is often also a hobby. Unfortunately, the financial barriers to entry (as I cited at the beginning of this section) are usually too high and too many.

On the other hand, in an MLM, you can get started in your own business for less than $1,000, usually less than $500. Not only are the opportunity costs for an MLM quite low, many other business costs are also eliminated through this kind of business venture. You don't have to worry about:

• Overhead
• Start-up Business Risks
• Customer Service
• Employees
• Employee Insurance

When I enroll a new person, I have a list of questions I try and ask. Two of them are, "How much money would you like to earn?" and "How much time do you have to devote to the business?" Some of the answers amaze me! There are people who want to earn thousands and thousands of dollars, and yet are only willing to put in a few hours a week. I quickly let them know that to earn a lot, you need to invest a lot of time. I help them create a more realistic plan so that their expectations of earnings versus time is well managed.

Knowing this, they can begin their business and know approximately what time will hopefully equal what profit. Remember (and I know this seems obvious, but you would be surprised how many people overlook it), to own a business you **must** make money. That means you need to receive more money than you spend. Keep close track of how much you are earning vs. how much you are spending. I have heard sad stories of people, across industries, who have lost tens of thousands of dollars before they even realized it.

There is no need to do that, so don't let that happen to you. Just like you budget your money at home, you need to learn how to budget your money in your new business. You will need some product, sales materials, and training materials, like this book, to guide you along the way. Although ongoing education is important, don't be fooled by people who may insist on you spending thousands of dollars on materials that you don't need or that can wait until later.

You are in the business of making money. I was taught something by the person who I think is the brightest in all multi-level marketing, Blake Roney, the Chairman and Founder of NuSkin. When I was their accountant, he pulled me aside one day and said, "Keith, there are two ways for us to make money. One is by the way and amount of what we bring in. The second is by how we spend what we bring in." He taught me the importance of, and how to wisely budget, each penny for the company. That piece of advice has helped me and the thousands of people I have shared it with. Even though it's not a groundbreaking concept, many people are of the spend-more-than-you-make mentality, which is one of the reasons we ended up in the "Great Recession."

It doesn't matter whether you are in MLM, a different business, or just trying to balance your own budget, you need to learn the art of saying "No." That way you can control your budget and your bottom line. Teach your downline or employees to always spend less than they bring in. It is the only way to run a lucrative business. In MLM, it is also important that you learn how to "bring it in." Study the compensation plan and then make an aggressive strategy on how to reach each financial milestone.

Legitimate multi-level marketing is based on selling products. Whether you, or members of your team, are selling the product, no one makes a penny unless a product is sold. With most MLM companies, every distributor can make money simply by retailing the products. A really good example of this is Mary Kay. Thousands of people have made a small profit by simply purchasing products at wholesale from Mary Kay and then reselling them to their friends and neighbors at a "retail" profit. Each distributor is like a miniature Macy's department store cosmetic's counter. They have product, they demonstrate its merit, and then resell it to the consumer. Transaction done and profit made. To make leveraged income, however, you need to bring in and sponsor new distributors. You need to duplicate your actions in others so that you can achieve leveraged income.

The more people you sponsor who sell products, the more money you'll make. The more people that your downline members sponsor who sell products, you will also make more money. In any compensation plan, Sales, New Members, and Duplication are the three keys.

Closing the Deal

I have spoken about bringing in more money. By this, I mean closing the sale and signing up a new distributor. Let me begin by giving you some important keys. The closing process begins long before you even meet with your first prospective client. There are three things you must do for a presentation to work.

#1: Feel the Part

It begins with your mindset. I can't count on my fingers and toes how many times I've seen a distributor psych him/herself up to not close the sale. They are positive they are going to be rejected long before they've even met the client. Of course, since their heart isn't in it, their self-fulfilling prophecy comes true, and they are indeed, rejected. Part of making the sale is actually acting like, and believing (there's that word again) that you're going to close the prospective customer. Before you pick up the phone, make the appointment, and meet the prospect, make sure your head and heart is in the right place.

#2: Look the Part

Are you dressed for the occasion? Do you look like the person you would like to work with? It's amazing how much your physical presentation will affect your verbal presentation. Tony Jeary, the speaker and author once said, "People who have presence are not simply prepared for a single moment— they are prepared to meet all presentation opportunities that arise in their lives."

Each person you meet is a "presentation opportunity" so putting your best foot forward at all times is necessary in this field of business. Remember, you can never make a first impression twice. Make sure you're smiling and keeping eye contact when necessary. A genuine smile and an open demeanor will get you into more doors than a fancy watch or expensive name-brand clothes. Also, stand up straight and walk with purpose. The way you hold yourself will illustrate to people whether you're confident or not. Most of all don't cross your arms, fidget, or look at your watch— you've just lost the sale if you let people know their time with you is limited and unimportant.

#3: Speak the Part

As you begin talking to someone, you need to start with the "end" in mind. The "end" is for them to say YES to join your downline or to buy your product. Because of this, as you present, don't come off being too pushy. Nothing will kill a sale faster than sounding like a "used car salesman."

Don't rush the sale or talk too fast. A good rule of thumb to follow is to match your speech rate to whomever you're speaking with. Also, remember to enunciate or speak clearly. Mumbling your presentation only tells your audience that you're not confident in the company, the program, or the product and that you have nothing great to say about it, which both you and I know is not true!

Also, make sure you choose your words wisely. What you say is as important as how you say it. Always select positive phrases. If there is a "problem," call it a "challenge." A purchase or sale is an "investment." A "downline" is a "team." How you say things makes a HUGE difference in how people perceive the opportunity.

People can tell the difference between a person who is out to make a dollar and a person who is out to make a difference. Be informative, helpful, and attentive so they can make an intelligent decision. Learn to listen to their questions and let them know that they are valid questions. Make sure you answer them to the best of your ability. If you can't remember, go back and review the common reasons a person may say no. (See Rule #2)

If you have done your job correctly, the person will usually join. If a person says "No," politely ask them why. Usually it's a good reason and you'll have a quick solution for it. However, this is MLM and even when you give it your best, you may hear a firm, solid "no." Always take the success and rejection in the same stride and learn from each experience. The final point in closing the sale is vitally important. Some years ago, a survey was done on people who had said no to a recent opportunity. The number one reason a person didn't join was that they were never asked to join in the first place.

Make sure that in every presentation, whether long or short, whether good or bad, you ask for the sale. Invite them to be a part of your team or to become a retail customer of yours. Always ASK for the sale! Knowing that you are involved in a business is a truly wise "Rule." Treat your business like a business. Bring in more and spend appropriately. Abide by the "Rule" and a better "bottom line" will be your reward.

How Are You Running Your Business?

Look at WORKSHEET # 3. Remember the key to this "Rule" is to realize and remember that you are in a business for yourself and to make a profit. In order to make a profit, there are two main points to remember with respect to your money, 1) how you make it, and 2) how you spend it. When I was in the University studying accounting and finance, they taught me over and over again the importance of budgeting money. For example, you may be earning $2,500 a month in your earnings, but the important number is how much you make after expenses. If you are spending $1,500 to earn $2,500, then you probably need to make some changes in how you're doing your business or spending your money. Yet, you can't make any significant and meaningful changes unless you know these three things:

1) How much you are earning.

2) How much you are spending.

3) What items you are spending money on.

In today's world of technology, it's easy to keep track of these categories. Remember, not only is it important to keep close track, but it's also the law of the land. WORKSHEET 3 shows you how to make a budget and follow it. First, you need to study your compensation plan and any promotions your company offers. Project the growth you will have in both your personal sales and group sales. This will help you estimate what your commission check will be.

Be realistic and make sure you are setting and achieving new goals; aims that will cause you to reach new earning heights. Personally, at the beginning of each year, I write down the amount of money I plan to receive in commissions. To do this, you need to know the compensation plan. If you need help, talk with your upline or a company representative. Decide on how much you believe you will receive; then try to project how much you will receive each month. For example, in January maybe you project a check of $1,000; February $1,500, March $2,000, etc. List each month out beneath the receipts section.

Also at the beginning of each year, try and determine how much you will spend each month. In many MLMs, you will buy product each month, purchase company training DVDs and CDs, and attend company conventions. To the best of your ability, try to place the expenditures under the month in which you will spend them. As I bring up expenditures, remember to save for taxes. One of the biggest mistakes distributors make is that they don't save for taxes and they don't send it in on a quarterly basis. Don't forget the taxes, the IRS likes to get paid! Learn to live within your budget!

The difference between the receipts and the expenditures is your net income. Each month, compare your monthly income to what you have budgeted it to be and what it really is. Make changes where you need to.

Worksheet #3: Budget

Receipts	January	February	Difference
Commission Checks	$1,200	$1,000	$200
Promotions	$50	$100	$50
Total Receipts	$1,250	$1,100	$150

Expenditures			
Advertising	$25	$75	$50
Product	$150	$100	$50
Travel	$50	$125	$75

Keeping track and entering items into your program is important. This worksheet shows when you are spending too much and where. Additionally, it shows whether or not your checks are growing.

MLM is one of the greatest ways to establish wealth. Why? Because it incorporates residual and leveraged income. Additionally, you should be able to get started at a fraction of the expense of what other conventional small businesses cost. You are your own boss and you are also the greatest employee you have! Knowing this, go out, sell yourself and the company, and make what you're truly worth!

Now It's Your Turn!

Receipts	January	February	Difference
Commission Checks			
Promotions			
Total Receipts			

Expenditures			
Advertising			
Product			
Travel			

Jack Yianitsas' Laws Of Success

The great sin – Gossip.

The great crippler – Fear.

The greatest mistake – Giving up.

The most satisfying experience – Doing your duty first.

The best action – Keeping the mind clear and judgment good.

The greatest blessing – Good health.

The biggest fool – The man who lies to himself.

The great gamble – Substituting hope for facts.

The most certain thing in life – Change.

The greatest joy – Being needed.

The cleverest man – One who does what he thinks is right.

The most potent force – Positive thinking.

The greatest opportunity – The next one.

The greatest thought – God.

The greatest victory – Victory over self.

The best play – Successful work.

The greatest handicap – Egotism.

The most expensive indulgence – Hate.

The most dangerous man – The liar

The most ridiculous trait – False pride.

The greatest loss – Loss of self confidence.

The greatest need – Common sense.

Step Four:
NEVER QUIT

Setbacks are a Part of Life

Don't let your fears or past failures derail you from having success. Setbacks are a part of life and sometimes they can actually put you on the road to wealth. The actor, Mickey Rooney said it best when he said, "You always pass failure on the way to success." Failure is a natural part of the success process. You just need to learn how to accept it, overcome it, and grow from each obstacle.

By the time I left NuSkin, I had already made my millions in the MLM industry and had done very, very well in the computer, real estate and bridal industry. Many people thought I would probably retire in style and enjoy a life of leisure. They were wrong. I believed in MLM, and what's more, I believed in work. I found out very quickly that I was NOT the "retiring" sort.

Since I had never done it before, I wanted to succeed as a distributor. Ever since I learned about MLM, I have been convinced that it is the best way to share and sell products from one person to another while accumulating wealth. So when I told people that my goal, after leaving my prestigious job at NuSkin, was to become a distributor, some laughed at me and others thought I was just teasing. Yet, I was very serious about it. Very serious.

I can still remember the day I first signed up as a distributor. The night before, a good friend of mine, Seth Moulder, called to see if I would be interested in hearing about a new MLM company he just joined. I didn't really want to. I didn't think he could have found a company that I would want to join. How could a twenty-five year old discover a company that even the former Sr. V.P. of NuSkin hadn't heard of? I admit, it was a moment of arrogance and I'm embarrassed to have felt that way. I reluctantly agreed when he asked if he and his upline could come over and try to recruit me to their company.

The next morning they arrived early. As they began to explain the compensation plan and company structure, the old flames of excitement and vision were again stoked in me. By the end of the pitch, I was ready to sign on the dotted line. Right after I finished my signature, before the ink even dried, Seth quickly took it to the company, whose headquarters were about five miles away. He was so thrilled with his new team member, he didn't want to give me the chance to have any second thoughts.

While he was getting my distributorship settled, another member of my upline asked me if I would go to California for a 3-4 day tour of several cities. I thought that since I had joined, I might as well get to work right away. So I readily agreed and thus began my start in MLM as a distributor.

While we flew to California for the first meeting, Seth and others were busy on the internet and phone. They were contacting people to let them know I was coming. By the time we got there, over 200 people were waiting for the meeting and me as a keynote speaker. For a company that had very few members, I was surprised by the size of the audience.

As I entered, two people rushed up to me and asked if they could film my presentation. Their goal was to sell it to help others just getting started in MLM. The pressure was mounting and by that time, I was becoming a bit nervous. As the audience continued to grow, the meeting began. One person spoke for about 5 minutes and then one of my new upline members stood and introduced me, saying a lot of nice things about me and building up a huge expectation for the crowd. By then, I was a nervous wreck.

What happened next will be forever etched in my mind. Over 200 people were on the edge of their seats expecting an uplifting, 30 minute talk about the merits of the company and why they should join. I walked to the front of the audience and said, "Hello. My name is Keith Halls. I joined this company today. Ummm, I think you should too." I stood speechless for about another 5 seconds. I swear a tumble weed blew past. Then I just said, "Thank you" and walked quickly back to my seat. At first, people thought I was joking, but within 5 minutes the room cleared. So many people left dumbfounded and disappointed. Never had so many people been expecting so much and gotten so little!

After my dismal performance, I quickly located the audio and video crew who taped me. My sole goal was to get that horrible video back. I was imagining what all of my friends would say if they got a hold of my presentation. I asked the two guys, who were so eager to tape me before the event, if I could buy it back from them. The main guy just handed over the tape and said, "Dude, we couldn't even give this away!"

Pretty awful, right? Wait, because it gets worse. Way worse. My upline, who had been so happy and excited for me to come on the trip, approached me afterwards. She said, "Keith, I know you're a very busy man and must have a lot of things to do back home. Why don't you just head back home today and I'll take care of the rest of the trip." Slam! Not only had I looked like an idiot in front of a couple hundred people, but now my upline, the one person I was supposed to look to for help, basically told me that I wasn't needed and I was on my own.

I agreed that going back home was the right decision, I mean what else could I say? I felt like a complete failure. It was raining that night when I caught a taxi back to the airport. It seemed like the longest ride and that every drop of rain on the taxi's roof was telling me that I was a failure and that I should quit while I was ahead. I knew that some rather unflattering things would be said about me and the story of my performance would quickly spread like wildfire. "Keith Halls joined and quit the same day!"

Many thoughts raced through my mind on that return flight home. Did I think of quitting? You bet I did (unfortunately). I mulled over all my options, but ultimately the decision I made that night, was that I would not quit. I would not let my hopes and dreams be stolen from me. I would figure out a plan that would allow me to succeed more than I ever dreamed possible. That night, October 1, 2002 was a long time ago. I cannot even begin to imagine how different my life would have been had I decided to quit.

Thomas A. Edison once said, "Many of life's failures are people who did not realize how close they were to success when they gave up." He would know too. The genius who gave us the light bulb, had infinitely more failures than he had successes. He was held back in school and his teacher labeled him "slow" and "unable to learn." He failed hundreds of times when testing the filaments in his light bulb. In spite of his failure, he held over 1,500 patents before he died and variations of his inventions like the light bulb and the alkaline battery are still central to our lives today! Imagine what would have happened if he had thrown up his hands in defeat on the first or second failure.

Like Edison, when I became a distributor the job was wrought with discouragement and failure. I think that many people in my situation would have quit. But I didn't. I was lucky enough to grow up in an environment where quitting was not an option and I am so grateful to my father and mother for it. I can still remember, at a young age, my father telling me that if I began quitting when things became tough, that it would quickly become a bad habit, which would then be hard to break. Often times, too many people quit when they hit a roadblock. Before you ever seriously think of quitting, think of the billions of other people who would be happy to be you and have your set of problems as well as possibilities. They would gladly change places with you in a second.

In order to succeed in MLM and in life, "Don't Quit" isn't just a good suggestion, it's one the "Rules of the Game."

6 Reasons _Not_ to Quit MLM:
1. A Fear of Failure
2. A Fear of Rejection

3. Worry over Peer Group Approval

4. Self-Doubt

5. A Desire to Remain in One's Comfort Zone

6. Acceptance of Mediocrity

There are times, however, when a person should legitimately leave a company. If any of these things are happening, you should seriously think about getting out. In these circumstances, you are not quitting, you are doing what is right.

5 Reasons to Leave:

1. The company is doing illegal things.

2. The company is not delivering products.

3. The company is not paying commission checks.

4. The company has lost its vision for the future.

5. The company changes the compensation plan too often.

Like the examples above, you must make sure that the company has quit you, before you quit them.

Also, there are other legitimate times when you might need to evolve or transform yourself. Maybe you are giving up something good only to get something that is infinitely better. That's not quitting, that's just being smart.

Wanting a new challenge, I left my first company as a distributor, and I joined another company. I knew the minute I ended my association with the former company and joined the new MLM, the check that I had worked so hard to build would also end. The residual and leveraged income I had built would disappear. Suddenly, I would have to start all over again and bank my hopes on a brand new company.

The first day with my new company, about an hour after I had signed up as a distributor, I got a call from my good friend Krista. She was a neighbor and we had been close ever since she had moved to Utah seven years earlier. She asked if she could drop by for a chat. When I opened the door, I could tell right away that she had been crying. We went into my office and began to talk. She told me that she had just lost her job. By all appearances, I knew that she did very well and earned a lot of money. We lived in an upscale neighborhood and she always had brand new cars, boats, and every toy you could imagine. She was 35 and very proud of her financial achievements.

Losing her job was a huge shock. She had 2 children and no idea what to do next. After talking to her for a while I asked if she had any savings? The answer was no. I asked if there would be any severance, and again the answer was no. I knew she needed money and she needed it quickly or she would lose everything.

I then asked her the magic question, "Have you ever been involved in MLM?" "No," came the reply. I told her that less than an hour before, I had signed up with a new company. I then told her why I believed that this particular company would be the right fit for her. Her dreams came with the sharp edge of immediate, practical demand. I sincerely hoped that my help would be exactly what she needed.

She looked at me and asked, "Can I really earn the money we need?" WOW! That was a loaded question. She needed to earn a lot of money and fast. I thought about it for a minute and then told her that I had seen some people earn a lot quickly, but she would need to talk to everyone she knew and work harder and faster than she may be accustomed to. She agreed. I then told her to stay up all night and think of people who might be interested in enhancing their health with our product while earning more money.

The next morning, I arrived at her house. Even though I had been kidding about staying up all night, she had done just that and compiled a substantial list. She had already arranged for two couples to be at her house at 8:00 a.m. to hear about an amazing new opportunity. They came, listened, and immediately signed up. We then told them to come back to the house in two hours and each bring two more couples to hear the story. They did and we repeated the process all day, everyday for over a week. Within a few weeks we were renting out hotel meeting rooms and packing them full.

Very quickly, her group grew to over 500 people! Krista and many members of her downline kept working. They began duplicating what they saw Krista doing successfully and by the end of 10 weeks, Krista was earning over $25,000 a month. It was MLM at its finest! She believed, she dreamed, and she worked hard. And, as a result of her tireless efforts, other people earned great returns too.

She didn't shut down when she lost her job. It would have been so much easier to do so, but she didn't. She had been at one of the lowest points in her life, but she pulled through, worked hard, and became an instant celebrity in MLM. She learned and applied what I taught her about the "Rules of the Game." Those rules were the very foundation to her success.

Once again, don't quit. Don't ever, ever quit. The famous writer, Henry David Thoreau once said, "Men are born to succeed, not fail." And that goes for the ladies, too! You were born to succeed, and you will, as long as you follow the "Rules of the Game."

Don't Quit for Peanuts

"Ninety-nine percent of all failures come from people who have a habit of making excuses."

- George Washington Carver

I believe that each and everyone one of us have been in situations where we would like to quit. We think quitting could and would make things so much easier. However, quitting, just like so many other things in life, can be become a very bad habit. I have watched as people have jumped from company to company, never staying long enough to experience the success they are so desperately looking for.

To truly understand the art of overcoming setbacks, appreciate just a small part of George Washington Carver's story.

By trying to help the plight of the poor people in Iowa, Mr. Carver was able to change the world. However, his life wasn't easy, by any stretch of the imagination. He grew up on a farm, a black man who had been adopted by a white family. His parents had passed away before he could talk. He grew up, smack dab in the middle of "Jim Crow" country. Yet, in spite of all this, Mr. Carver became one of the most brilliant men the world has ever known. He never allowed prejudices of others to deter him from his sense of self and his dreams. He never quit and the world is a better place for it.

By 1896, Mr. Carver became a professor at Iowa State University and was very famous for his study in the methods to helping plants grow. His work caught the attention of Booker T. Washington, the president of the poor, yet prestigious Tuskegee University in Alabama. Washington asked Mr. Carver to join their staff. Though Tuskegee could never pay Mr. Carver what he was worth, he was interested in helping poor black and white farmers. He accepted the invitation.

Prior to Mr. Carver arriving, Tuskegee had been gifted the 21 acres of land that adjoined the University. The land had not been fruitful and whoever had given the land to the University, probably thought it wasn't worth selling.

Mr. Carver decided to research the land through county and state records and found that the 21 acres had yielded below 25 pounds of cotton per acre. That kind of yield would be disastrous to any farmer and yet many farmers were having the same results close to Tuskegee University, as well as throughout the country. Why? The soil was worn out from years and years of growing cotton without crop rotation and proper care of the land.

In the summer of 1914, George Washington Carver, after studying fertilizers at great length, found that nitrogen was necessary to replenishing the soil with the many vital nutrients lost in overplanting. Mr. Carver discovered that the peanut plant, a plant with no known use, if planted in nutrient-deprived soil, would deliver the nitrogen that would quickly restore the soil to its originally healthy state. With this knowledge, he took those same poor performing 21 acres that had previously yielded only 25 pounds per acre and planted peanuts instead of cotton. The very next year, the soil enriched by the peanut plant, yielded over 500 pounds of cotton per acre!

The surrounding farmers, of course, were thrilled with the results and wanted to improve their own yield. They too restored their soil by planting peanut for a year. However, now the farmers were left with hundreds of tons of product with no known use. That meant the farmers didn't have a cash crop to sell for those years and with no cash, they had no way to pay the banks, feed their families, or buy cotton seed for the proceeding year. Suddenly the grateful farmers were furious with Mr. Carver and Tuskegee University. These angry white farmers, who were about to lose their farms, began demanding justice. And since Tuskegee was state-funded, all of the fuss from the farmers put the University's sustainability in peril.

George Washington Carver, without any foreknowledge of peanut benefits, told Booker T. Washington to make the announcement to everyone that within a week, he would have a solution to the peanut problem and would help the farmers.

Within a week, ONE WEEK, George Washington Carver discovered many uses for this once "useless" nut ranging from cooking oil to printer's ink. In 1916, he published, "How to grow the peanut and 105 ways of preparing it for Human Consumption." He saved the University, saved the farmers, and put the peanut on the map as a useful commodity.

Because one man did not quit, one of the world's most famous and favorite foods was found to have hundreds of uses. The farmers were saved and the next season, because of the increased nitrogen in the soil, the cotton crop yield set new records.

I encourage you to follow George Washington Carver's example and never quit. Always keep working and trying.

One of the best things that helps me is a "WORKSHEET" identifying the uses and the benefits I am receiving from the company, its products, and its compensation plan. This increases my belief and faith, and strengthens my resolve to never, ever quit. This is just a sample. I keep a separate folder for each topic and place everything I know and learn into it.

Worksheet #4: Never Quit

Company

- Helps people throughout the world achieve financial freedom, while enhancing their health.
- Employs scientists to keep up with the latest and greatest in science and nature.
- Implements ways to help make our products ecologically friendly.

Product

- Helps provide nutrients to people.
- Helps to lower blood sugar.
- Helps to regulate blood pressure.
- Provides the vitamins and phytonutrients that are essential to the body.

Compensation Plan

- Provides money quickly to new members.
- Provides a full time income to those who are willing to work as hard as they can.

Remember, you cannot quit and succeed; the words are completely incompatible.

Now It's Your Turn

List the benefits of your chosen MLM company here. If you're not in an MLM yet, list what benefits or reasons you need to see before joining a company.

Company

_____

_____

_____

_____

_____

_____

Product

_____

_____

_____

_____

_____

_____

Compensation Plan

_____

_____

_____

_____

_____

_____

"If you would thoroughly know anything, teach it to others."

– Tyron Edwards

Rule Five:
TALK AND TEACH
FROM THE HEART

Love What You Do, Teach What You Love

I have been actively involved in sales, in MLM and in other industries, for over 30 years of my life. I have been to conventions, heard countless motivational talks, and have been to numerous presentations. I would guess that in my lifetime, I've been to over 1,500 meetings.

The presentations that stood out and were well received were the presentations where the person was speaking from the heart. Rule #5 to live by is to teach from the heart.

When I owned a string of bridal stores, every Saturday morning, all the 40 or so employees from the parent store would attend a training session before opening the store that day. The number one rule we taught was to work from the heart. In fact, before a new employee could go onto the sales floor for the first time, he/she had to learn to apply that lesson and pass a test. The very best salespeople are those who sell a product or service that they truly believe in.

As I previously said, after I signed up as a Distributor, I didn't follow the "Rules." Why? I hadn't learned them yet. Sure, I knew some of them and believed in what I did know, but I didn't really put them into planned action.

After I had been a Distributor for less than a year, I decided to go back to Texas and reconnect with some of my old friends. When NuSkin went public, I became kind of a celebrity with my old crowd. I am positive that they were shocked beyond belief when they heard that the company, I was originally one of the shareholders of, had begun selling their shares on Wall Street. On November 19, 1996, we sold hundreds of millions of dollars in shares in just one day. All of those years of dreaming, building, and working as hard as we could, finally paid off beyond our wildest imaginings!

After going public, I had a lot of friends ask me to let them know if I ever got involved in another company. After my huge success with NuSkin, they would gladly become an investor or a distributor with any company I decided was worth my time and effort.

So, after many frustrating months as a distributor, I decided to contact many of these old friends via email and telephone. I began inviting them to hear about this new company. More and more people said that they would love to listen. So I carefully planned a trip to Texas. By the time I booked my flight, several hundred people had already told me that they would come to a presentation. I predicted we would have about 250 avid listeners, so I divided up the venues between Houston, Dallas, and Austin.

Can you imagine receiving emails from that many people saying they would love to hear you talk about something, anything? I was so excited that I asked one of my upline members from Boston and a downline member on my team to help me. I just knew that I would need help filling out all those applications and entering them into my downline.

We scheduled the first meeting in Houston, from there we would fly to Austin, and then we would finish in Dallas. On the first night, at 7:00 PM, we walked into the room to begin the meeting. I was expecting about 75-100, but when we entered the room that evening, there wasn't one to three hundred, in fact, there weren't even four people who had come. My balloon went pop! I couldn't believe it. My friends had told me they would be there. The same thing happened the next night in Austin. I had my best night on the final night in Dallas—there were 12 people in attendance, however, over half of them were already members. I was more than discouraged, I felt numb.

In my whole life, that weekend ranks as one of the top ten in embarrassment and humiliation. Can you imagine how it felt driving the two people to the airport who had come to help me? Talk about awkward!

After dropping them off, I decided to go to Nacogdoches, my small hometown in East Texas. My parents were still living there, and at that moment I needed a pair of friendly, welcoming faces. I didn't call, I just drove straight to their home some 200 miles away. When I entered the back door, my parents were delighted to see me, yet, they could see that I was very discouraged. My mother and I went to the kitchen table and sat down. After several hours, I had spilled the entirety of my discouragement to her.

My mother asked me to tell her exactly what I was doing. Up to that point, every time I had spoken to someone in depth about the company, I had pulled out my computer and gone over, in detail, my PowerPoint presentation. It had actually become the backbone of my presentation and the crutch I relied on to present. As I shared the story with my mother though, I didn't use the computer at all. She listened intently and told me that it was very impressive and she couldn't imagine why people wouldn't join. She asked if she could invite her friends to come to her house to hear what I had to say. When she asked that question, I cringed. I loved my mother, and couldn't bear the thought of her being rejected too. But she believed in me more than I believed in myself and was adamant, so I finally agreed. At that point, I went back to my old bedroom to sleep off the last few nightmarish days.

About an hour and a half later, she woke me up. She said that there were some people there to listen. I was ecstatic! I quickly put on my tie, got out my computer and projector and followed her into the living room. When I entered I was shocked! Sitting in front of me were about 25 ladies, all friends of my mother. The youngest was probably 70 and the oldest probably 85. I made a huge mistake as I began. I asked, "How many of you would like to learn about how you can obtain long-term income?" Their quick and witty reply was something like, "We would just like long-term!"

I fired up my computer and turned on my projector. I was doing the presentation by the book, just like my upline had taught me:

Dim the Lights
Turn Projector On
Read Presentation Verbatim

Everything was going smoothly until about 10 minutes into the presentation when I heard a soothing, restful sound. It was the sound of people snoring. I was so boring, that I had put many of them to sleep. I was the new answer to insomnia!

My mother then did something that would forever change my MLM life. She simply went over, turned off the projector and computer and said, "Keith, just tell my friends what you told me."

Ugh, I was now without my "mechanical crutch." After swallowing hard, I did what my mother asked me to do and for the next 40 minutes, I told them about the company I believed in, the products I personally used and why, and the money I made. I spoke with all my heart and they all saw it for what it was—a truly great business opportunity and program. By the end of the meeting, every lady there either signed up as a distributor or purchased product. Finally, SUCCESS!

After the meeting was over and the lovely ladies had gone home, my Mom asked me if she could share just a few ideas with me. Very humbly and gratefully, I told her "Yes, I would be very glad to listen to anything you have to say." She told me why she believed we had succeeded that day. The first reason was trust (see Rule #6) and the second reason was that I spoke from the heart.

The ladies had come to the meeting because they knew my mom and trusted her. They in turn trusted me because of the association.

She then said that the difference between the two methods I used when I talked with her friends and when I had previously spoken to others was night and day. When I used the Power-Point, I depended on the computer to tell the story. There was no feeling behind it because, like I said, I was in "mechanical mode." However, after she turned off the computer, I was left to speak to them, just like I had spoken to my mother, from my heart. She said that when you speak to people from the heart, they can "feel it." They're more likely to believe your story and want to be a part of whatever company and product that you're sharing.

Wow! Was she ever right! A few months later, I started traveling to Japan and Thailand to build my downline. I don't speak a lick of Japanese or Thai, so I would often have an interpreter. Unfortunately, interpreters speak with zero conviction and don't interpret the heart.

With this language hurdle, I quickly learned that the important thing for them was to look into my eyes and feel what I was sharing with them. The main thing about speaking from the heart is that the sincerity is already in the words as you speak them. Sincerity will create business and sales. Because I have learned to speak from my heart, I have had over 250,000 people (a very conservative estimate) join my downline.

No matter who you are or where you are, if you learn to speak from your heart, people will not only believe you, they will be willing to follow your lead. This "Rule of the Game" is a positive game changer.

Worksheet #5: Elevator Pitch

There are a lot of theories on presentations. Should they be long or should they be short? Should they give everything away, or just a taste? The correct answer is that you need to incorporate all, depending on the setting, in order to succeed.

Usually, people have no problem over-talking about the benefits of the company. In fact, too many people speak much longer than is really necessary to get the point across. With few exceptions, I believe that 45 minutes is long enough for an effective presentation; if it's longer, you will start to lose the interest of your guests. As you plan your 45 minute presentation, you need to make sure that you give all of the important information in an understandable and logical way. You need to captivate your audience and the only way to do that is by speaking concisely from the heart.

The hardest type of presentation to give is the short 2 minute presentation. In the "go-go days" of Silicon Valley, when computer technology was just gaining momentum, it seemed that everyone was writing computer programs or developing a new piece of software to sell. They all seemed to have one thing in common, they needed money. In order to raise the capital needed to fund their software or hardware company, many of these entrepreneurs turned to Venture Capitalists (VC). One of the biggest problems was that the Venture Capitalists had only so much time and couldn't possibly listen to everyone. The entrepreneurs who truly believed in their project, but couldn't get time with a VC, came up with a new idea. They would design a presentation that was only 2 minutes long. Why? Because they figured that they could go to the VC's elevator floor and ride down with him or her. That gave them about 2 minutes of time. They had to sell the VC's on their company and idea in a very short elevator trip down to the parking lot. This became known as the "Elevator Pitch."

If you are going to make a short presentation, you can only cover the most important points and present them straight from your heart. Write down the points and then write out your script. Practice it so that you can speak with confidence and conviction. Practice your presentation in front of a mirror or tape yourself giving the presentation. Listen to what you are saying and put yourself in other's shoes. Would you, if you were them, believe what you just said? Would it interest you? Would you want to know more? If the answer is yes, then you're ready. If the answer is no, then keep practicing.

For Worksheet #5, list all of the key points you need to cover in your elevator speech. The following is an example:

1. Our company is fully funded.

2. The product is changing the lives of others.

3. The compensation plan works.

4. There is a training system that will benefit everyone.

Remember, this "Rule of the Game." It is essential and will allow you to touch people's lives and capture their imaginations. When you have done that, you have won the sale!

Now It's Your Turn!

Write Your Two-Minute Elevator Speech. Remember to state who you are, what you know, why you know it, and why it's important for them to know it too.

_____

_____

_____

_____

_____

_____

_____

_____

_____

_____

_____

_____

_____

_____

_____

_____

_____

_____

_____

_____

_____

_____

_____

"Trust is a peculiar resource; it is built rather than depleted by use."

–Unknown

Rule Six:
TRUST

The Trust Factor

Webster's Dictionary defines the action of trust as:

a : to place *confidence : depend* <trust in God>
   <trust to luck>
b : to be confident : *hope*

MLM was designed around the very idea of trust. At its core, it's built on the foundation of interdependence— simply put: what I do or don't do affects you, what you do or don't do affects me. Because of this, it fosters a very close knit community of people striving for not only their own personal success, but also the success of others. Goals and benchmarks are intertwined and any outcome, whether good or bad, is ultimately shared by many. The good of one, is essentially the good of all!

Trust can only be built with steadfast and ongoing effort, and one slip up can cause days, months, even years of backpedalling.

One mistake can be incredibly damaging.

Let me give you an example of a time when a personal oversight severely violated a strong sense of trust I had with my father.

It was Spring, 1978. I was still living in Texas attending the local university. A group of about five or six of us decided to celebrate Spring Break together. We were all good students, had studied hard to keep up our grades, and desperately needed a break. We decided to go boating. My father had recently purchased a boat that was only few years old and in excellent condition. You could use it for both waterskiing and fishing and my father loved it. It was his pride and joy. He trusted me enough to let us borrow it for the entire Spring Break. We spent the days waterskiing and camped by the water at night. It was the fun in the sun that we needed after all those grueling hours at school.

We decided to celebrate our last day on the water with a case or two of beer. I seldom drank but it was the last day and I wanted to join in the festivities. Some girls, who had come up for the day, went to buy the beer while we cleaned up the camp site. Our goal was to get everything ready so we could just go home after a day of skiing.

I did something really stupid that day that I had never done before, nor have I done since—I drank, knowing full well that I would be the one driving later. We didn't have a designated driver; we were all just designated drinkers. We thought it was a great way to end such a great trip.

Because we had all been drinking, none of us were thinking clearly. As we were packing up all the gear to come home, we forgot to do one very important task; we overlooked the safety straps which attached the boat to the trailer.

As we began the 30 mile drive home, I turned left to get out of the parking lot. The momentum caused the boat to flip off the trailer. As bad luck would have it, we happened to be next to a very steep embankment and the boat rolled to the bottom. Several cars stopped to help us bring up what was left of the boat out of the embankment. My father's boat was totally and completely destroyed.

We were a middle-class family and that boat was a huge purchase for my Dad, who loved to fish and take us kids waterskiing. As I was driving home, my stomach hurt with the guilt of knowing that I had destroyed one of my father's happiest hobbies and the thought of it was unbearable. By being so selfish, I had ruined one of my father's favorite past times.

Along the way home, we stopped by a little stand that was selling bar-b-que. We needed to mask the smell of the alcohol. We each ate a sandwich and then, for good measure, bought a side dish of sliced raw onions. I wasn't sure what I was going to say, but I didn't want my Dad to smell the alcohol on my breath.

When we arrived at my house, all of my friends quickly ran to their cars and left as fast as they could. They didn't want anything to do with the trouble that was most assuredly on its way.

I trudged into the house and meekly asked my father to come outside. I can still remember, that as he walked outside, he was smiling. When he saw the broken boat, the smile disappeared immediately. He walked around the boat just staring at it, his mouth agape with utter disbelief. He didn't say a word. His dreams of fishing were utterly destroyed. At one point he stopped, reached his hand into the broken boat and pulled out an empty beer can. He turned to me, looked at me hard for the longest 20 seconds of my life and said, "Here, you forgot to hide this one." He then walked back into the house without saying another word. I knew that the trust he had in me, which I had fostered over a lifetime of being responsible, was seriously shaken. There could not have been a worse punishment for me than the look on his face and the disappointment in his stooped shoulders as he turned his back on me and slowly walked into the house.

That night, and for many nights after, I went to bed sick with guilt. I had spent a good part of my life trying to impress my father. I wanted his approval and I wanted him to be proud of me, and here I was, a Sophomore in college, an adult, and I was suddenly messing it up. I felt that I lost the thing I wanted most from him—his trust. He was a good man and even though he didn't completely lose his trust in me, it was seriously compromised for some time.

A few years later, after NuSkin went big, I flew home and took my father to buy him a brand new, deluxe boat. I was finally able to give him back his favorite past time. He never asked for it, but the smile on his face, when I handed him the keys to his brand new boat, was priceless!

Under the previous "Rule," I told you the story about my mother teaching me the merits of trust. She said, "Trust is one of the very hardest things in the entire world to gain. Trust is also one of the easiest things to lose. One wrong action can possibly harm or destroy a lifetime of good works."

Your Word is Really All You Have

I would like to tell you a story about the man I refer to as my "brother," Mr. Kaneko from Japan. In my opinion, he is one of the greatest distributors in MLM. He works harder than most, believes in the company and product, and has so much compassion for his downline team. All of these qualities translate into a very accomplished and successful business man.

In early 2003, about 6 months or so after I became a distributor in MLM, I began traveling to Japan to recruit new distributors into my downline. I talked tirelessly to countless people, but wasn't having any luck. The fact that I didn't speak Japanese was making the endeavor rather difficult! Mr. Kaneko had learned that I was there trying to attract new distributors for the company. He knew about me from my NuSkin success and couldn't imagine why I would have traded my prestigious position, working for such a large and esteemed MLM company, to climbing down the corporate ladder to work as a distributor.

One night, while I was in Japan, the President of the company I was a distributor for, was also in Tokyo. He was hosting a dinner to thank the few distributors we had in Japan for our service and effort. When I arrived that night, I heard that Mr. Kaneko and Mrs. Ichigawa were also there and I quickly introduced myself. Mr. Kaneko and Mrs. Ichigawa were in the publishing business and did a lot of work for MLM companies, so while they knew about my history in MLM, I also knew about theirs. They said that they had come to this dinner in particular, to learn why a former Sr.V.P. and Member of the Board of NuSkin had decided to come to Japan as a distributor. It was such a unique story that they were thinking of writing a book about it.

After dinner, I had the chance sit down with them. We chatted about our mutual interest in MLM and I told them that the reason I left the MLM big leagues to join the little leagues was because I wanted to fulfill a dream of mine. I wanted to create leveraged long-term residual income.

Since I would be leaving the next day, I promised them that I would return to Japan shortly and that I would love to speak with them again. They were quite shocked when I really did come back. You see, many Americans will promise to return to Japan or Taiwan, but rarely come back. On the return trip, I met with them several times and tried to convince them to join my downline. Our talks went well, we enjoyed each other's company, and the time spent together flew by. We developed such a good friendship and working relationship, I just knew they would join right away. I promised them that if they joined, I would do anything and everything needed to help them succeed. As my trip came to a close, I still had not persuaded them to join, so I went home empty handed and a little disappointed. After our many talks, I knew they had what it took to prosper in an MLM environment.

After flying home from Japan, I landed, got my luggage, and began my one hour drive from the Salt Lake Airport to my house. As I was driving and thinking about my recent experiences in Japan, I got a phone call from the president of the company. He said, "Keith, you told them you would do anything. He wants you back here tomorrow or the next day."

I had been gone from my family for over 2 weeks, I was tired, and a little bit jet lagged, but for me, my word is the most important thing I can ever give to someone. I knew that I needed to return to Japan. I had begun building the groundwork of trust between me and Mr. Kaneko and Mrs. Ichigawa and could not risk those weeks of hard work by not following through on my promise. So I called, booked a ticket to Japan, turned the car around, and went back to the airport. That one action, solidified the trust they had in me and swayed them to join immediately.

Within a few short months, we had thousands of new members in Japan. Why? Their association with me opened the floodgates and with that trust, we were able to recruit thousands. We made a great team and more importantly we made a lasting friendship. We became like family to each other.

If you want to succeed in MLM, and more importantly, if you want to succeed in life, you need to learn how to build and maintain trust in others. There is no other way to succeed. This "Rule of the Game" cannot be overlooked. Work as hard as you can to obtain trust and teach others to do the same.

Worksheet #6: Trust

In MLM, as well as in life, you need to be able to establish trust between yourself and others. All relationships are based on trust. It makes a marriage work, it's the foundation of a parent/child relationship, and every boss trusts his or her employees to do what they say they will do, when they say they will do it. It's exactly the same in MLM. The people whom you sponsor need to trust you. Your downline must believe that you will help and support them in their milestones toward success.

Worksheet #6 will help you develop trust with your downline. Keep a list of promises you are willing to make to the members of your downline. Give the list to every person whom you sponsor, so that they know your seriousness and willingness to help them succeed.

Also, in the "Promises I made, Promises I keep" column, list all of the promises you have made. By listing all of the promises you make, you can often refer to the list and make sure you are fulfilling what you said you would do. I left two spots open for you to fill in some of your promises and how you plan to keep them.

Promises I Make / Promises I Made	What I will do to fulfill the promises
1. Help recruit at least one downline.	1. Make a list of the new person's member contacts.
	2. Call the first 10 people together.
2. I will stay in close contact with my downline.	1. Call my downline 3 times a week to train them.
3.	
4.	

Naturally, the list could go on and on. It will help you stay accountable to yourself and to the people you promised your time and resources to.

One of the biggest reasons a person doesn't sign up with you is that you haven't been able to establish a relationship of trust. Until you do this, you will not succeed.

"A good listener is not only popular everywhere, but after a while he gets to know something."

- Wilson Mizner

"Never doubt that a small group of thoughtful, committed citizens can change the world. Indeed, it is the only thing that ever has."

- Margaret Mead

Rule Seven:
ASK FOR HELP

Help and Be Helped

"Every great man is always being helped by everybody; for his gift is to get good out of all things and all people."

- John Ruskin

Help! I need help. Beyond a shadow of doubt, if we want to succeed in MLM, or any business venture for that matter, we need to learn to ask for help. For most people, asking for help is extremely challenging. Some think it's a sign of weakness—no one wants to look incapable or dependent, right? But I encourage you to put aside all of those negative associations about asking for help. If you want to succeed, you must let down your guard, eliminate your pride, and learn to ask for help. I believe that one of the key factors that kept me from succeeding back in 2002, when I first became a distributor, was that I was unwilling to ask for help. Not only was I unwilling to ask for it, I was unwilling to follow in the footsteps of others. I thought, how could the former Senior VP and member of the Board of a Billion Dollar MLM giant ever need to ask for help from anyone else? What would people think if I needed help? I can now admit that it was a huge mistake of pride on my part.

Helping Hands

In my office at home, I have a white clay figurine of two hands clasped together in a praying position. I initially bought it to remind me to take time to pray on a daily basis, which is very important to me. It still serves that purpose, but there is also a very touching story behind this particular piece of art.

During the 15th century outside of Nuremburg, Germany, there was a goldsmith who had 18 children. The father usually worked 18 hours each and every day just to put food on the table. Two of his sons had a dream. They wanted to become artists. However, they knew that their father would not be able to help them financially achieve this goal.

The two brothers put their heads together and came up with a solution that would help them both achieve their artistic aspirations. One of the brothers would go to the Art Academy in Nuremburg and study, while the other would go to work in the local mines. With the money that the brother working in the mines earned, he would support the other brother financially while he attended school. After the first brother was done with the Art Academy, they would switch places and he would go to work at the mines, while the other brother would have his chance at the Academy.

To decide who would first attend the Academy, they flipped a coin one Sunday after Church. The winner would get to go to the Art Academy and the loser would go to the nearest mine and begin supporting the other. Albert Durer lost and went to the mines; Albrecht Durer won and attended the Academy.

Albrecht became an instant success. His paintings, etchings, woodcuts, and water colors were far superior to many of his professors. By the time he graduated, he was already being commissioned to do art work for others. He had already made a name for himself and was seen as a rising star in the art community.

True to the promise he made to his brother, after he finished and graduated from the Academy, Albrecht returned to the small village where his family lived. Upon his return, his father threw a feast to welcome him home. At the end of the meal, Albrecht stood up to raise a toast to his brother and thank him for his long sacrifice in the mines, which allowed him to go to the Academy. At the end of the toast he said, "And now, Albert, blessed brother of mine, now it is your turn. Now you can go to Nuremberg to pursue your dream, and I will take care of you."

At the other end of the table, Albert had his head down and tears were dropping into his lap. After several minutes of silence and anticipation, Albert stood and said, "No, brother. I cannot go to Nuremberg. It is too late for me. Look, look what four years in the mines have done to my hands! The bones in every finger have been smashed at least once, and lately I have been suffering from arthritis so badly in my right hand that I cannot even hold a glass to return your toast, much less make delicate lines on parchment or canvas with a pen or a brush. No, brother... for me it is too late."

To pay homage to Albert, Albrecht Durer carefully drew his brother's broken and battered hands with the palms together and his thin fingers stretched toward the sky. He called it simply "Hands," which others later renamed "The Praying Hands." These broken, helping hands of his brother were the main reason Albrect's hands could become the tools used to create so many world-known masterpieces.

Albrecht Durer is still considered one of the world's most famous artists. His works are found in nearly every major art museum in the world. But his most famous work of all is the one he called "Hands." It is a symbol of love and sacrifice. The sculpture was designed to remind us that success only comes with the help of others.

The Evolution of Help

When we were children, we would never hesitate to ask our parents, with a sincere heart, for help. Our parents would gladly give it to us. But by the time we hit high school, we rarely, if ever, asked anyone for help. We progressed in the art of being independent. We wanted to be free to make our own decisions, and in one way or another, we rebelled so we could live on our own terms. We didn't want to be seen holding onto mom's "apron strings." Unfortunately, it's these formative years when we had so many important questions and because of a fear of looking weak or uncool, we rarely asked them. The results were often poor grades, frustration, and bad decisions. By the time we entered the work force, we usually only asked questions during the training sessions. After that, because of pride or fear, we kept the questions to ourselves.

If you want to succeed in life, you must learn to ask for help. This is such a vital "Rule of the Game." MLM can be hard enough as it is, yet when you're loaded down with frustration and you're stuck and need help, but you're unwilling to ask for it, success cannot happen. That's right, if you don't learn how to ask for help, you will not succeed.

Part of the key to this rule is that the person you ask to help you must be willing to do so. Can you imagine asking your upline for help and having them respond, "No." Or worse, saying yes and then never following through with it. Before you join an MLM Company, you must find out more about your upline members. How involved are they in your training and success? Are they willing to take some time to show you what they've learned works and doesn't work? Do they ultimately care if you're a part of the team? If there is any reason for you to believe that they're not interested in you completing your success milestones and will not help you, then you should not join that team. If you suspect it's a chronic problem in the company as a whole, then it's time to move on to another MLM. It really is that important.

Another key point is to learn that when others are trying to help you that you need to carefully listen to their advice. Always remember, you can never listen yourself out of a job, but you can talk yourself out of learning valuable information. When in the company of a successful MLM member, remember to do less talking and more listening.

Too many people in our industry believe they need to reinvent the wheel in their business. You don't need to go through all of that effort. Instead of reinventing, learn to follow in the footsteps of those who have paved the path to success for you.

Many years ago, when I was making well over $100,000 a month as a distributor for Synergy, I received a call from a new and rising distributor. He had ambitious goals and I admired him for that. The problem was, he wanted me to take some time out of each day to train him on what works and what doesn't. I had over 200,000 downline members and it was impossible to personally help each and every one of them. I tried to be generous with my time, but in cases like this, I would usually refer them back to the person who enrolled them. If that upline member couldn't or wouldn't help them, then I would quickly get involved.

However, this young man insisted on my personal help. It wasn't that I didn't want to help him, but my schedule was heavily booked. I worked approximately 18 hours a day, 7 days a week. A huge chunk of my business (about 90 percent) took place in Asia, so I had to get up early every morning to read emails and make phone calls. I told my young friend that if he truly wanted my help, he would have to be available at 3:30 a.m. It was the only time I had left in a day.

He took on the challenge and set his alarm for our 3:30 a.m. calls. As a result, I worked hard to help him succeed. He went on to become a huge success. He said that the time I spent with him during those early morning trainings helped him tremendously in his career. He sacrificed his sleep, I sacrificed my time and the effort paid off!

Asking for help is a vital "Rule of the Game." Don't just ask for it, learn to follow it also. Teach the people you recruit into your downline to also ask for help. The result will be a more confident and efficient team.

Worksheet #7: Asking For Help

As you begin your MLM journey, write down the areas where you know you will need help. Next, be sure to give your upline a copy and make sure they are willing to help you. Remember, working with your upline is the beginning of the duplication process. It is not a sign of weakness; rather it is the sign of someone who wants to succeed.

If you are already in an MLM company, share this method with your downline members and ask them to fill out an "Upline Support Wish List." Then instruct them to do the same for their downline members. The result will be a community of people working in concert to help each other succeed. Here is a simple example that you can use to devise a list of your more challenging areas in MLM and who can help you with the solutions.

Areas I Need Help With	Upline Member Who Can Help
1. Inviting people to meetings	Mary
2. Learning more about the product	John
3. Best scripts to use on the phone	Lisa
4. Ways to advertise	Mary
5. What markets are the best to approach	Mary

Now It's Your Turn!

What areas are you struggling with? Who can help you reach your personal milestones toward success? Use this form to figure it out.

Areas I Need Help With	Upline Member Who Can Help
1.	
2.	
3.	
4.	
5.	
6.	
7.	
8.	

"A good objective of leadership is to help those who are doing poorly to do well and to help those who are doing well to do even better."

– Jim Rohn

"A kind compassionate act is often its own reward."

– William John Bennett

Rule Eight:
BE KIND AND HELP OTHERS

I Met a Tumor on the Way to Success... And I'm a Better Person

For It It's been over 20 years since I had a life altering experience. I was practicing for a mini triathlon and was very excited. I knew I wouldn't win, but winning for me would be just finishing the event. It was a dream of mine; a very big dream.

You see, when I entered Brigham Young University, (remember this was my second degree), I did not weigh anywhere close to my high school weight. Then, as I got deeper into the accounting program at BYU, I saw a whole lot of desk time and rarely any activity time. By the time I was 25, the fruits of my "desk-labor" were quite evident. All my studying, working, and eating lots of junk food, combined with no exercising made me quite fat. Not just a little bit fat, a lot of bit fat!

To graduate with a degree from BYU, I had to take and pass a class called "Fitness for Life." Let me just say that this class was an "exercise in humiliation." At the beginning of the term, they tested your body fat and then you worked closely with your teacher and assistants to improve your fat-to-muscle ratio. At the end of the term, they tested you again, and the difference between the two was your grade.

The first day I measured obese. Ouch! They told me that if I didn't change my ways, I would probably die from a heart attack by 35 or 40. Now that's one way to motivate someone! Unfortunately for me, I took the class during Summer Semester, which was about half the schedule time than a normal semester. With less time on my hands, I had to work harder to get a good grade. It was a much needed wake-up call and the reason why I made it a goal to compete in a mini-triathlon. I knew that the kind of regimen that goes into training for a triathlon is the kind of regimen that would get my accounting-softened butt into shape!

In the beginning, I developed a habit; I would run 6 days a week for at least 3 miles. I began to take care of myself and watch my calorie intake, and soon the pounds began to fly off and all aspects of my life improved. I had to lose those pounds before the real triathlon training could begin. It took some time to get to the training stage, and by then, I had graduated from BYU and was already working at NuSkin.

At this point, things were going so well in my life. NuSkin was already in full momentum and our success story was rippling through the MLM community. I was married, had two wonderful children. My life was pitch perfect. It seemed as if life was too good to be true, which I was about to find out, that it was.

In a triathlon, there are three different events that you have to compete in: biking, swimming, and running. I did my bike training early in the morning so that I would have time later in the day to train on one of the other events. I did this almost on a daily basis.

After a while, I started having challenges with balancing on my bike. In the middle of a ride, I would simply fall over. At first, I thought I was just really clumsy, or since it was early in the morning, that I was still groggy from waking up. Regardless, it was really embarrassing. After falling, I would quickly get up and brush myself off. I always acted like I had hit a bump, so in case people had witnessed my total goof up, they wouldn't worry about me or think I needed to buy some training wheels.

Also, during this period in my life, I became easily confused about my location when I was biking. The same thing was happening when I ran or swam. Before long, I started getting severe headaches on a daily basis. Although my body was getting stronger, I felt like my mental abilities were getting weaker.

One day, I became so confused as to my whereabouts. I walked into a local convenience store and told them I was lost, gave them my driver's license, and asked if they would please call my wife. I was a grown man lost in my own neighborhood. Right after that frightening episode, I immediately went to the doctor's office. I had already been several times before complaining of headaches, but this was an entirely new and disturbing development—I felt like I was losing my mind.

The doctor scheduled an MRI for the next day. Late the night after the procedure, I got a call from my doctor. He simply said, "Keith, we have found some abnormalities on your brain. I have scheduled an appointment for you tomorrow morning with a neurosurgeon; don't miss it." I slept very little that night.

The next morning I went to the neurosurgeon's office. He placed the photos of the MRI on a screen where I could see them. He pointed to an area of my brain and gently broke the news by saying, "Keith, these two circles are tumors. Now, we need to remove at least one of them. The one we will remove is in an area where the chances for problems are much less than where the other one is." He then said they would remove it and perform a "freeze test." From what I understood, the freeze test was about 95% accurate in ascertaining if the tumors were cancerous. If the first tests were positive, he would then need to remove the second one. Unfortunately, the second one was in a more dangerous spot, where many sensory nerves were located. The chance of losing one or more of these nerves was quite high.

I was stunned. At first, I didn't feel fear, I was angry! How could this be happening to me? Why was it happening right now when I was at the top of my "game?" The doctor gave me about a week before he performed the surgery.

Word spread quickly throughout our community. I didn't want the attention; I just wanted to be with my family. But because of my position at NuSkin, I needed to make sure that everything was in order and my daily tasks were assigned out. Because I was making preparations for a month-long absence, word spread like wildfire through the office.

Over the course of the next few days, many of my friends came to our home to let me know that they were praying for the best outcome. One of my "friends" came to my office. I greeted him warmly, thinking he had come to wish me a quick recovery like everyone else. However, after a brief conversation, I quickly realized that his intentions were of a totally opposite nature. I sat stunned as he walked down the hall from my office to the NuSkin's Chairman's office. Here I was, scared witless about my mortality, and he was putting his name in as a replacement for me. That hurt beyond belief. I thought I knew him. I was going through one of the toughest and most terrifying times in my life and a so-called friend was taking advantage of me and my situation.

Eventually they did hire me another accounting officer who worked closely with me during this period of time. He's a man I truly respect, and for my sake, I'm glad they hired him. When he started, he had no knowledge of my challenges. He was, and is, a truly honorable man and friend. (Thanks, M.E.).

I'm happy to report that the surgery was a huge success! After I recovered, I met with NuSkin's Chairman and asked him why he hadn't replaced me with my friend? He was better educated, had a lot more experience, and to be honest, knew a lot more about accounting than I did.

The answer surprised me. He said, "Keith, in the very beginning, one of the biggest reasons I wanted you to be a part of the team was because you were always smiling, you were always friendly and kind, and you worked so hard. I knew I could ask you to do difficult, time-consuming tasks that most people would complain about or do only half way. But you would always answer me with a smile and then get the job done promptly and effectively."

A smile. Just a simple smile. I made millions of dollars with an imperfect smile that never had the benefit of braces. A single smile and a positive attitude landed me in the position to be associated with a mega-company who has helped many other people. A smile changed my life and kept me in a wonderful job!

My smile and positive attitude also opened doors for me into other realms of business. As NuSkin was just beginning, a good friend of mine asked me to help him with a computer company he had recently formed. He had written a code that made part of the "LAN technology" possible. For my part in the company's growth, he would give me stock in a company that had a 17-year life on a patent that we also received commissions on. I didn't write one word of code. I barely even knew how to turn on my own computer. Instead, I helped him by communicating with companies, like IBM and Intel, who used his product. He was incredibly smart at computing, but lacked the time to sell or talk about his code. At a crucial point of my life, I was fortunate enough for him to choose me to help. Why did he choose this non-technical guy? Because I would smile, and go out of my way to be nice to others. I made sure that he and the company were running smoothly and lucratively and that his clients were satisfied with the service. The company did so well financially, that I felt embarrassed about how much money I had earned and ended up returning the stock he had given me.

Once again, a smile, a good attitude, and a staunch desire to help others launch themselves into success made all the difference.

Be nice, be kind and learn to help each other. This is not a utopian request, this is one of the "Rules of the Game." It's a crucial rule of success in both MLM and life. I definitely would not have had the success I've had without abiding by this rule.

We live in a world that is becoming increasingly narcissistic by the day. It's a "me first" society. I have heard the "What's in it for me?" mantra so often, and each time I do, it makes me cringe. I don't suggest that you shouldn't be careful or that you shouldn't make sure that your family, livelihood, and personal health are taken care of. But when we put ourselves first, above all else, we are on a slippery slope to unhappiness.

When I was failing at the beginning of my career as a distributor, I was not going out of my way to put others first. As I look back now, I can see that the person I was the most concerned about was me. However, the minute that I quit worrying about me, my progress, and my check, and I began to reach out and help others succeed, my success as a distributor was enhanced tenfold!

Some of you may read this "Rule of the Game" and think that it's so simplistic, or that I'm simply repeating the Golden Rule. Although most know it, very few apply it. Few "Rules" could ever help you have more success, than simply being kind and helping others.

The Golden Rule is especially important in MLM. How you treat others will come back to either haunt you or bless you through your downline. If you consistently train and encourage your downline to achieve more success and better results, you'll find that the fruits of your labor will continually multiply. If you teach them through a constructive and productive example, you will create a positive feedback loop that will continue to duplicate. On the other hand, if you ignore your downline, you'll find that it will become barren of growth and lacking in exceptional talent. In MLM, you truly reap what you sow!

How Do You Rate on the Likeability Scale?

I enjoy reading the news and since my first degree was in Political Science, I especially like to stay abreast of politics. I like to read local, national, and international political news. Many times, I look for the latest "popularity index" of politicians or other prominent figures. Most of the politicians are trying to make sure that their popularity numbers are high, especially during an election season.

Let's imagine now for a minute or two, if there was a "likeability index" in your home, office, neighborhood, and downline? What if there was an election today? Would you be elected for a second term? What if everyone was given the chance to vote on a scale of 1 to 100, 100 being the highest vote? Your friends, associates, employees, coworkers, family members, and downline could give out as many 100's, or in the same vein, as many 20's or 30's as they deemed you deserved.

If we held that index today, how would you rank among your neighbors? Your friends? Your downline? And most importantly of all, how would you rate with your family? Would it be 80 or 40, 90 or 30? Be honest, as Mark Twain said, "You can't lie to yourself."

If the result is that you scored in the 80s or 90's, you've probably lived a good life and people enjoy your company. Most people like to be around you and they will listen to you and want to follow your example. Which means you're definitely MLM material! Your chances for serious achievement are incredibly good and many will cheer you on as you move up the ladder of success.

Remember, people will follow those who are considerate and compassionate. Nancy Reagan once said, "I am a big believer that eventually everything comes back to you. You get back what you give out." If you want to be blessed, learn to bless others. It will improve all aspects of your life.

Life passes by too quickly. However, instead of being sad about something you can't change, learn to use your time effectively. You can change the way you act and treat those around you and learn to treasure every minute. By doing so, you will find more happiness and you will become a better person.

Kind Acts Are More Important Than Kind Thoughts

Another part of the "Rule" is to put kindness into action. We may think about the nicest, kindest actions and although our intentions may be incredible, our actions are negligible.

As I've mentioned before, I travel much of the time. Often when I travel overseas, I find tucked inside my suitcase 10-20 hand-written letters from my wife. On the first night, I read the letter marked #1, the next night the letter marked #2, and so on. I am always so grateful for these sweet remembrances from home and this small and loving action by my wife truly draws me closer to her.

Yet, I have only reciprocated this action for her a handful of times. Before I go, I think about making her small notes to read every night while I'm gone. I have such great intentions, followed by negligible actions! If she only knew of all the sweet things I am thinking about! For example last summer, I intended to spend at least two hours each day, and the weekends with my family. However, I didn't quite succeed in this lofty and thoughtful goal. Even though my kids say it was the greatest summer ever, I could have done better.

Just as my family can't read my mind, your friends and downline can't read yours. You don't get credit for thinking nice things, you only get credit for doing nice things. Our good intentions must always be put into action.

What often separates the best-liked, most successful people from the mediocre, normal people is that they always put their good intentions to work. They don't just think, they DO! We can't intend ourselves to success. To succeed, you must abide by this "Rule" and remember that it requires ongoing action.

Be nice, be kind, and help each other! It's that simple!

Worksheet #8: Acts of Kindness

Worksheet #8 can help you immensely throughout your entire life. This worksheet lists some actions you can take to become the nicest, kindest person you can be! I left some blank spaces for your ideas. This one "Rule" can make you be the kind of person that others will want to follow.

1. Learn the birthdays of all the people you sponsor and send them a birthday card.
2. Write a real live letter "snail mail" to your downline members telling them how much you appreciate them.
3. Pay for someone's dinner in a restaurant. Don't let them know that you did it.
4. Tell your downline you appreciate them.
5. Have a weekly "Family Night." Turn off the television and other distractions and just be with them.
6. Write a letter to your company thanking them for all they do.

Now It's Your Turn!

Now, you add to the list and then GO AND DO IT!!!

1._____

_____

_____

2._____

_____

_____

3._____

_____

_____

4._____

_____

_____

5._____

_____

_____

6._____

_____

_____

"An idea that is developed and put into action is more important than an idea that exists only as an idea."

– Buddha

*"Knowing is not enough; we must apply.
Willing is not enough; we must do."*

– Johann Wolfgang von Goethe

Rule Nine:
WORK AND ACTION BRING RESULTS

Just DO it!

All of the Rules we have talked about are vitally important for your success. However, even if you followed all of the first 8 Rules, you would not achieve true success if you didn't actually go to work. WORK. Yes, that four-letter word applies to MLM too. You must actually implement and put these "Rules" into action for any sort of measurable success to take place!

I am constantly amazed at how many people think they can join an MLM Company, work a few hours a week, and then expect thousands of dollars for it. Work doesn't "work" that way! It's called netWORK marketing for a reason. Not only must you work, you must also learn to overcome the common obstacles associated with MLM. Thomas Fuller once said, "All things are difficult before they are easy." The same thing applies to Network Marketing. Each and every one of us will be faced with roadblocks and hurdles. There will be days, or even weeks, when you don't sponsor a new member onto your team. There will be times that you may find it hard to keep your downline motivated and duplicating. These difficulties, or difficulties just like them, will most assuredly arise along the way, but it's your job to overcome them. Sometimes it will seem that the harder you work, the more obstacles you'll stumble upon. Let me just encourage you by saying that from personal experience every stumbling block is actually a stepping stone toward success and your reward will be residual, long-term income.

First Thing is First, Get Over Yourself!

When I first started writing this book, my goal was to reach out and help people in this industry succeed. Another goal for writing this book was to teach you how to get out of your own way and into the way of financial freedom. To do this you must get off your couch and approach the millionaire you know and invite him or her to be a part of your team. I know, you've put them on some untouchable pedestal, and you think that they would simply poo-poo the very idea of MLM, but let me tell you a secret. I speak with millionaires and professionals almost every day. They're faced with the same exact dilemma many people are facing, which is "How do I obtain or maintain an ongoing paycheck now and into the future?" Many of these millionaires and professionals have said to me, "Keith, I am making a lot of money right now, but want to retire some day. I need to find something that gives me continual, residual income for the rest of my life." See, they are not so different from you or me, right?

On September 30, 2002, a 27 year old named Seth Moulder called a millionaire he knew. I know he was scared, but he called and guess what? The millionaire joined. The company was able to match a rather large portion of the checks of the people he sponsored. So, that millionaire went to work. It wasn't success at first go, but the millionaire became a $100,000 + a month income earner. And Seth was probably making close to $40,000 to $50,000 a month. I know this story very well because the millionaire was me. As you get to work, take this book to all of the professionals and millionaires you know and ask them to read it. I know they are looking for residual, leveraged income and you can show them the way to earn it! Get to work and share this wealthgenerating knowledge with them!

The Obstacle in Our Path

In ancient times, a King had a boulder placed on a roadway. Then he hid himself and watched to see if anyone would remove the huge rock. Some of the King's wealthiest merchants and courtiers came by and simply walked around it.

Many loudly blamed the King for not keeping the roads clear, but none did anything about getting the big stone out of the way. Then a peasant came along carrying a load of vegetables.

On approaching the boulder, the peasant laid down his burden and tried to move the stone to the side of the road. After much pushing and straining, he finally succeeded. As the peasant picked up his load of vegetables, he noticed a purse lying in the road where the boulder had been. The purse contained many gold coins and a note from the King indicating that the gold was for the person who removed the boulder from the roadway. The peasant learned what many others never understand.

Every obstacle presents an opportunity to improve one's condition.

Perseverance: It's the Best Tool of the Trade

Many years ago, I got a frantic call early one Sunday morning from my sister. Her 10 year-old son, Cory, had been shot in the head, a victim of an accidental shooting. Cory was lifeflighted to a prominent hospital in Salt Lake City, where they told her that he was not expected to live. That Sunday morning, on two separate occasions, the doctors operating on Cory came into the waiting room to tell us that he had passed away. Both times, within minutes, they came running back to tell us he had survived. Miraculously, Cory made it through the first night. For the next 6 months, he resided in the hospital and most of that time he spent in a coma.

Cory had to have part of his brain removed. All of us were broken hearted for him, my sister, and my brother-in-law. All of us wondered what kind of a life he would have. Would he recognize us? Would he be able to talk, to read, or live something that resembled a normal life?

I was amazed and proud of the hundreds of hours my sister spent helping him in physical and occupational therapy. Gradually, he recovered enough to go back to school. Each and every assignment was a struggle and they worked with him every night at home. Cory, who had been through so many brain surgeries, made the honor role in high school. If I look back on all the times I made the honor role in high school, I come up with a big fat 0. I didn't take advantage of my opportunities to learn, and I was too lazy to do the work. Yet, here was my young nephew teaching me how to work hard and overcome seemingly impossible obstacles. He even went on to attend a university and is now working at a great job. All of the miracles were only possible because of a very kind God, an incredible boy, and a tireless, persevering mother, my sister Sally.

The Merriam-Webster dictionary defines perseverance as: *"Continued effort to do or achieve something despite difficulties, failure, or opposition."*

Too many people quit when the going gets tough and never realize that the fruits of their labor are very close to being realized. Never allow the rough spots to define the whole of your career in MLM. I promise that they are only stints, momentary blips in your life, and that if you continue to work, you'll find yourself in a better, more lucrative place. As William Feather, an American author and publisher, once said, "Success seems to be largely a matter of hanging on after others have let go." So, just keep hanging on!

The Path Has Already Been Paved...
The Steps Have Already Been Mapped Out

If you want to succeed, follow the path of those who have succeeded before you. That's why I'm giving you the roadmap to MLM success here. I've been there, done that, and know what works. Every item I list in this next section is meant to aid you and keep you focused and determined on your journey in MLM. You can also find a copy of these worksheets at *www.KeithHallsAcademy.com*. Even though these are not all-inclusive steps, I've listed the most important actions necessary to get you started on the path to success. Each time you complete one, check it off.

Whenever you sponsor someone, always give them a copy of these steps. They will be key in helping you facilitate the success of your downline. Remember, it's a work in progress and these are not all of the steps. Add any that you discover along the way and keep developing the list. Your downline will be miles ahead because of your commitment! Always remember that a smarter downline is a more profitable downline.

Before You Join

In the MLM world, there are literally thousands of different companies. Before you decide on an MLM company, seriously consider what type of a company you want to join. There are both large and small companies, and there are companies that pay using a binary tree, while others use a unilevel tree. There are even companies that use both. Some companies will have you purchase a lot of inventory up front, while others won't.

Before you join, list out all the things that attract you to an MLM company and make sure the one you choose can meet most, if not all, of your criteria. By doing so your decision-making strategy will be clearer.

Here are some ways to gain clarity in this decision making process.

1. Learn everything you need to know about the company, so you can make a wise decision and be proud of it.

2. Learn about their products. Sample them, research them, and make sure they are something you feel good about selling to others. If you don't like or trust the product, you'll never be persuasive in the sale.

3. Read up on the history of the founders and major players in the company. Know who you'll be working with, both directly and indirectly.

4. Learn about their compensation plan and how it will benefit you both short-term and long-term.

5. Talk with your closest family members and make sure they are supportive.

6. List the dreams you want to accomplish from being a part of an MLM company. Write how you plan to accomplish them.

RULE 9: WORK AND ACTION BRING RESULTS

Your First 48 Hours

Your first 48 hours can be the most important hours in your MLM career. If you are already in an MLM company, then the next 48 hours can be the most important. During these hours, you establish your base and you put yourself on the right track. Now that you are a member, work closely with the person who sponsored you. Ask them to help you with the following tasks. If you have just sponsored someone, share these steps with them and let them know you're on board 100 percent to help them fulfill these tasks.

1. Fill out the company's application for membership.

2. Pick the right auto-ship or monthly package.

3. Pick the right start-up kit for you.

4. Write down your why and how.

5. How much money do you hope to make?

6. How many hours are you willing to work each day? Each week?

8. How do you access the back office trainings and information?

9. What are your upline's phone numbers?

10. When are the company's training calls? When are the "team's" training calls?

11. Make a list of at least 50 people you want to work with.

   a. Business builders

   b. Consumers

12. Learn how to invite someone to hear about your company.

   a. Write out a 30 second "invitation"

   b. Memorize it

   c. Practice it in front of a mirror

13. Find out where the meetings are held. Always bring at least 2 new people to the meetings.

14. Find out the different ranks of leadership.

15. Write down when you will achieve each rank.

16. Meet with your upline or the person who sponsored you.

    a. Give them a copy of your dreams and goals.

    b. Schedule times for weekly (or more often) calls.

17. Work diligently with your upline.

18. Sponsor two people.

Your First Week

1. Make a budget.

    a. Include how much you are willing to spend by category, i.e. products, travel, phone, etc.

    b. Open a bank account for your business.

    c. Save money for taxes and learn how and when to pay.

2. Make folders so that you can track your income and expenses. Keep all of your receipts and place them under the correct category.

3. Study about your Company for at least 15 minutes a day.

    a. Company

    b. Products

    c. Compensation Plan

5. Access your back office and use it as a tool.

6. Call 5 people a day to just say 'hi.'

7. Attend the local meetings in your area. Always invite two people.

8. Work with your upline

9. Work with your downline.

10. Present your company to at least five new people each day.

11. Give a copy of this book to each person you sponsor.

How Do I Help My Downline?

1. Find out the dreams and goals of each person you sponsor.

2. Help your downline sponsor at least 2 people.

3. Give each person you sponsor a copy of this book.

4. Give each person you sponsor a PDF of these steps.

5. Call each person twice a week.

6. Ask them what you can do to help them.

7. Teach them the success system you use to attract people.

8. Host a promotion. Promotions generate excitement.

9. Go to lunch or dinner with the people you sponsor.

10. Hold a "Dutch Treat" meeting at a restaurant. The more you are together, the more you will develop a good working relationship with like-minded individuals, and the more likely you will all succeed. Make sure everyone brings at least two guests.

Start Today!

The steps above are a worksheet of ideas that will help you and your downline. Naturally, these lists are not conclusive.

There are many other steps. You will learn some, you will be taught some, but the most important thing you can do, is to take the information and put it into action immediately. Not tomorrow, not next week, and definitely not next month! Start the process TODAY!

Only by applying this "Rule" of action, will you ultimately succeed. If you plan on making MLM a full-time commitment, then you must work hard and devote time to the effort.

I think of my personal doctor and lawyer. Both of them attended years of advanced schooling, and then worked very hard to achieve their licenses. With the power of MLM and residual and leveraged income, and by working hard, I am able to earn more than both my doctor and lawyer combined. Do you think I was able to do it without working? The answer is obviously NO. However, by working effectively and efficiently, by working an extra hour or two each day, I have been able to achieve what I set out to accomplish and much, much more. And I believe, with these "Rules" you can too!

Success in business requires training and discipline and hard work. But if you're not frightened by these things, the opportunities are just as great today as they ever were.

– David Rockefeller

FINALLY: IT'S YOUR TURN TO SUCCEED

The Rules of the Game are the Rules to Live By

Well, I have given you 9 of the "Rules of the Game." These are not 9 Suggestions, these are Rules. Your success in MLM and in all fields of your life will depend upon how well you can implement these.

Let's quickly review each one:
• Rule One – Dream the Dream
• Rule Two – Believe
• Rule Three – MLM is a Business; Treat it Like One
• Rule Four – Never Quit
• Rule Five- Talk and Teach from the Heart
• Rule Six – Trust
• Rule Seven – Ask for Help
• Rule Eight – Be Nice, Be Kind, Help Each Other
• Rule Nine – Work and Action Bring Results

Everyone wants to succeed, but not everyone has the roadmap and "Rules" to success. With this guide, you're miles ahead of many people still struggling to make it out of the rat race.

You now have the passport, the map, and the desire to enter a new, more sophisticated race… the one to residual and leveraged income!

You're at the starting line and with these 9 "Rules of the Game," the finish line is much closer than before!

Now you need to train your downline on the "Rules." Can you imagine how different your results will be once everyone in your downline is implementing these "Rules?" Can you imagine how much more effective and profitable your team will be?

For over 25 years now, I have succeeded in MLM—on the corporate level, as well as on the distributor side of things. I know that these "Rules" can change your results, your income, and most importantly your sense of happiness and peace.

Write down all 9 of the Rules, and put a copy of them on your computer, in your purse or wallet, by the mirror in your bathroom, and any other place you frequent to constantly keep you focused and mindful of your goals. Incorporate them and make them part of your daily life.

MLM is the most effective way to share products and help people earn the extra money needed to support their family. It's also the most effective way of creating long-term wealth.

Success is just within your reach. Follow the "Rules" and go and reap the rewards!

"When things go wrong as they sometimes will;

When the road you're trudging seems all uphill;

When the funds are low, and the debts are high

And you want to smile, but have to sigh;

When care is pressing you down a bit-

Rest if you must, but do not quit.

Success is failure turned inside out;

The silver tint of the clouds of doubt;

And you can never tell how close you are

It may be near when it seems so far;

So stick to the fight when you're hardest hit-

It's when things go wrong that you must not quit."

\- Unknown

Who Is Keith?

Keith Halls is one of the very few, if not the only person in all of Network Marketing to earn well over $10,000,000 on the Corporate side; then turn around and do it all over again, earning millions upon millions as a Distributor. He has earned millions as a distributor with not just one, but with two MLM Companies.

Keith was raised in Nacogdoches, Texas. He attended Stephen F. Austin State University where he graduated Cum Laude with a major in Political Science. He also attended Brigham Young University where he got a B.S. in Accounting. Keith is a non-practicing CPA.

In 1986 he joined NuSkin full time and was one of the 7 Original Shareholders. He was also a Senior Vice President and a Member of the Board Of Directors. He was part of the team that helped NuSkin in their Initial Public Offering in November of 1996.

In 2002, Keith became a Distributor in Synergy Worldwide and was the leading distributor in building an international organization of well over 200,000 members. In 2008, he became a Distributor in Exfuze where he once again built a large international organization. He has received numerous sales awards from both companies. Keith has also been successful in the Computer, Real Estate, and Bridal Dress Businesses. Keith and his wife Heather are the proud parents of 6 children: Christina, Rebecca, Mark, Michael, Erica and Matthew and one grandson, Logan.

SUCCESSES WITH KEITH HALLS

Keith is the greatest leader in MLM we have ever seen in our 20 year history. His teaching and training have helped people all over Japan succeed.

Nobuhiro Kaneko, Tokyo, Japan

Since the first time I spoke with Keith, he has made me feel confident that success is attainable in the industry of network marketing. He is the type of leader that I strive to become.

Aline Kafentzis, CA, USA.

Keith has taught us to do whatever it takes to help our business grow. We have met thousands and thousands of people in this business, but never anyone like Keith. Keith's experiences, knowledge, and success that he shares are enough to help millions to millions and millions more succeed. I believe everyone who wants to be successful in this industry should read and use this book."

Lek Sasipa Praditponlert and Aim Pathamarat Tonjunpong, Bangkok, Thailand

Keith Halls is indeed an amazing example of success in networking; both as a corporate head and then in the trenches building a business. If networkers had more of his qualities, more of them would be successful AND the world would be a better place. Keith Halls is a great man and a great example for us all.

Joan Harker, Canada

If you want to do this business with integrity and heart, just follow Keith's advice like I did.

Caroline Conlan, PA, USA